My Journey to Mongolia:
A Reporter's Journal

By Charles S. Rice

Table of Contents

To those with a sense of adventure

Thanks to Eric Schwartz

With special thanks to the Knight International Journalism Fellowship Program

Prologue

For me, Mongolia was always one of those faraway places that I looked at on a map and thought, "This place is remote." That all changed for me in the summer of 2002, when I applied for and (much to my surprise) received a Knight International Journalism Fellowship to Mongolia.

As a mid-career journalist at the Associated Press, I would be sharing my experiences with Mongolian journalists over a nine-month period beginning that following June.

It was considered a "backpacker fellowship" which meant I would get to see virtually the entire country. I could hardly wait.

While I had traveled in parts of Europe and Asia, it would be the first time that I would be living outside the United States. I began to read anything I could find on Mongolia. The more I read, the more excited I became, but I freaked a bit when I started reading up on those extreme Mongolian winters. How would my body react to 35 degrees below zero? What would I do to stay warm if the heat and electricity go out? What does one do during those long winter days and nights?

I had to cope with all of those questions during my time in Mongolia and began writing dispatches to friends and family about my adventures. Many of them suggested that I compile these dispatches into a book and that's what you are now holding in your hands.

As I worked on this manuscript, one question that I kept asking myself was 'would this book be relevant after nearly a decade after leaving Mongolia.' The short answer is "yes." Most of these stories are timeless -- focusing on relationships, culture and human nature. Occasionally, there are references to places – namely restaurants and bars

– that may no longer exist, but I have included them because they are relevant to the larger story.

There are also occasions where I felt it necessary to offer updated information to you, the reader, and this is provided at the end of the story. In one case, for instance, I describe flying on a particular Soviet-era aircraft. This aircraft has since been relegated to history and now is a museum piece.

Over the past half dozen years or so, Ulaanbaatar, the capital, has gone through dramatic changes brought on by a gold, uranium and copper rush – turning this remote outpost into a boom town. In Ulaanbaatar, or UB for short, dozens of new restaurants, bars, shopping malls and hotels have gone up – as have prices.

Yet, a part of the Mongolia that I experienced remains and it is that part on which I focus in these stories.

My nine months in Mongolia turned into a year and four months and by the time I departed, I had visited 17 of the 21 aimags (provinces) that make up this land-locked country sandwiched between Russia and China.

My Journey to Mongolia: A Reporter's Journal is a compilation of short sketches of incidents, usually written shortly after they occurred. They offer a glimpse of my 16 months backpacking across the Mongolian steppe training journalists -- where I met reindeer herders, feasted on sheep ears, bonded with Eagle hunters, drank fermented mare's milk, hiked through a blizzard and awoke to an icy hotel room to discover my toothpaste had frozen. All along the way, I met some of the warmest people in the world in one of the coldest places on Earth.

First Days in Ulaanbaatar

The cab driver is zigging and zagging through the streets of Ulaanbaatar at top speed. I am looking for a pattern to this traffic, but there appears to be none. Red lights and stop signs are ignored as are traffic lanes and pedestrians.

I've never been afraid of traffic, but suddenly I am frightened – really, really scared. I realize it would be easy to get hit and no one would seem to care.

I don't even consider crossing Peace Avenue, the main street in the Mongolian capital. I've noticed those brave enough to attempt it get half-way across before they're stuck in the middle of the street with cars fanning their clothes. I've seen a few even get whacked by car and truck mirrors.

One middle-aged lady carrying milk in a large see-through plastic bag was bumped by a car and her bag exploded – milk burst from the bag – covering her and the ground.

Traffic in UB is absolute chaos.

At first glance, there appear to be no rules of the road.

Collisions are common. It's no wonder many of the taxis have cracked windshields. It is best, I am told, not to sit in the front seat of a cab – always slide in behind the driver. It's safer. As one Mongolian told me, "if there's going to be a crash, the driver will do everything possible to protect himself."

It's advice that I heed.

I've been in UB for just four days now and I'm thinking that one day soon I will have to face this new fear – and actually cross the street. This is what's occupying my thoughts as my driver slowly pulls up to a wood-framed building where I will hold my first journalism workshop. It is being held in a place called Russian Restaurant, inside a little hotel called Edelweiss on the southeast side of the capital.

I am speaking this morning to seven Mongolian government officials – including three prosecutors, a Supreme Court official and one journalist. One of the prosecutors has driven 60 kilometers to attend my workshop on writing successful press releases. I'm told that this will be the first time that a foreign reporter will hold a workshop for government officials.

My thoughts of crossing traffic have faded and now I'm getting a bit nervous about the workshop. Will I live up to their expectations? What are their expectations? Am I prepared? Will the guy who drove 60 kilometers think he has wasted his time? All these thoughts are running through my brain and then suddenly, when I begin to introduce myself – I settle down. I know this stuff. I have lived and breathed it since I was sixteen and got my first radio job back home in North Carolina.

It's going to be OK.

The goal of this workshop is to demonstrate how short and concise press releases can be used to attract the attention of journalists who are looking for a good story to cover.

After a briefing on how to create a press release, I give each of them writing exercises and then each assignment is critiqued. The group is attentive, cooperative and asking lots of questions. They are particularly interested in how American journalists use press releases. I emphasize that press releases are rarely used word for word – but are instead used as a springboard to a story idea. That is apparently not the case in Mongolia, where government-issued press releases appear regularly as "news stories" in the local papers.

I prefer to work only with journalists, particularly on a topic such as press releases, after learning that press releases are often printed "as is," but this workshop had been arranged before my arrival in Mongolia. It would have been awkward to have refused to take part in it – and after all, one guy had traveled 60 kilometers of really bad roads to show up.

As I step outside the Edelweiss after the workshop, straight ahead, a dozen or so kilometers away, I can see the mountains that surround this city. It is my first clear glimpse of them since my arrival. Until today, the view had been obscured by smoke from dozens of forest fires raging to the north in Russia. The sky is blue and a gentle breeze is blowing.

As I take in the view, I forget about Ulaanbaatar, or UB, as the expats call it – a seriously neglected city. Weeds are growing everywhere and litter seems to sprout from the bushes and undergrowth. Animal bones are scattered upon the ground. Cars are belching black and blue smoke. Peeling paint is a trademark on many of the buildings.

The filth turns my stomach. It will be difficult to eat here for fear I will get sick. Yet, hunger always wins – and somehow, I set aside my fears and disgust and actually find myself diving right into the UB restaurant scene.

My first night, I had soba noodles, at a new Japanese restaurant owned by a Member of Parliament. Lunch the next day was delicious Turkish kebabs served with bread, raw onions and tomatoes on the huge porch of the Opera House that faces Sukhbaatar Square – the plaza in the city center. Dinner was Mongolia grill at a beer garden. Tonight, it was a tasty chicken gyro in a tidy little place on the first floor of what used to be KGB headquarters during the Soviet period. As I walked through the gate, on the right side, I noticed a little guard shack.

I let my imagination tinker with this fact. How many people passed through this gate on their way to interrogations for violating the Soviet system? Where are these people now?

As an American, we were fed some serious propaganda about the Soviet way of life – much of it true, but how much of it was just manufactured? No doubt, the KGB did some pretty nasty stuff as did their western counterparts.

These first hours and days in Mongolia, I find myself becoming fascinated with the remnants of the old Soviet system: the old work slogans, in Cyrillic lettering, still glow at night from atop the buildings in the city center; the drab identical-looking Soviet apartment buildings that seem to stretch forever; the Soviet car brands like Volga and Lada; even the red lights that go from red to amber to green rather than green-amber-red;

I've traveled quite a bit outside the United States and, of course, one notices that each country has its own way of doing things, but, here, it's like a completely different system – a system that is slowing fading away as Mongolia opens its doors wide to everything Western – including our style of journalism.

Author's Note: Traffic remains a huge problem for Ulaanbaatar motorists. It can take nearly an hour to travel less than five miles in the city.

June 18, 2003

Fresh Air and Training Journalists

Claude Monet would have loved it here. I am walking through a mountain meadow covered with thousands of wildflowers. I have never seen so many colors – blue, orange, red, pink, purple, yellow. As I admire these brilliant paint strokes, I am reminded that nature has to work fast – Mongolia has one of the shortest growing seasons on the planet.

Off to the right, perhaps 300 yards away, is what is believed to be an ibex – a four-legged animal that resembles a deer. My hiking mates tell me it is rare to see the ibex in this part of Mongolia since they've been hunted almost to extinction. Overhead, ravens float on the wind – and at times squawk – sounding like sonar aboard a submarine. It is a bird sound that I have never heard before.

This meadow reminds me of pictures of meadows in the Alps in Switzerland. And while it is just 30 minutes from UB, it is a world away from the belching smokestacks and noisy traffic of the capital city. The meadow is several hundred feet above the city – and occasionally, through the trees, I can see UB in the distance.

We are doing an 11-mile hike through Bogdkhan National Park. At times we are hiking through birch groves where someone has stripped the white bark from sections of the tree trunks. I am told that Mongolians tap these trees – just like sugar maples – to gather the sap to make a sweet wine.

As my hiking mates and I make our way through the meadows, the birch trees and the stands of evergreen trees – we are passing dozens of ovoos. These are large piles of stones or wood piled in a circle. Within these cairns are all sorts of gifts – money, bottles of alcohol, candies and even milk.

Ovoos are religious sites used in Buddhist ceremonies and also for worshiping the mountains and the sky.

When possible we walk to the left of them. Normally, a person is supposed to walk around an ovoo – clockwise three times – in order to have a safer journey. I figure it can't hurt and do the requisite three times around. I feel a bit dizzy afterward.

Here in the hills above UB, the air feels clean and the light wind makes the hike pleasurable after a busy week.

I had conducted my second journalism class - a three-day workshop for 20 or so Mongolian journalists - and welcome this outing. Most of the workshop participants had traveled great distances to get to the capital – up to 1800 kilometers. They ranged in age from about 21 to 67. The workshop was titled "Covering the Courts." I began with a short lecture and opened it up for questions.

I was peppered with questions for nearly 90 minutes. Many of the participants wanted to know if Hollywood films accurately portray what happens in real courtrooms. Others wondered if executions were broadcast on television. Some asked if America was less free since September 11th because of the public safety versus civil liberties debate.

I answered no, no and yes.

Most of the workshop involved writing exercises. We held mock trials and then the reporters were asked to write stories about the proceedings. I spent a lot of time removing opinion that kept creeping into their stories. There was also a lack of attribution – and in some cases they called the suspects "convicts or criminals" before the suspects had even been convicted. Other times, the main news nugget was buried in the last paragraph of the story.

Perhaps this sounds naïve, but I was a bit surprised by this style of journalism. Having spent nearly 20 years with The Associated Press, I had experienced elements within stories that occasionally leaned toward personal opinion and judgment, but nothing on this scale. It was eye-opening and I quickly realized this was exactly why I was here – to try to share what I had learned with them.

Yet this style of journalism is probably a natural outgrowth of the Soviet system – where reporters had been forced to censor themselves and now suddenly they can say and write almost anything.

Day two was much better. It was rewarding to see that their stories improved in such a short period of time. As I walked into the room that morning several people told me they were eager to have their work critiqued.

The third day was very interesting: a trip to an actual courtroom. We visited two courtrooms of the district courthouse in UB. Both rooms contained a computer and an audio recording device that captured every word of each trial. It was installed by a U.S.-funded American-based non-governmental organization that was working to reform the judicial system. Its mission is to place these recording devices in every courtroom in the country to create a transparent court system.

Courthouses equipped with computers allow the public and reporters to view exactly where each case is in the judicial process. There's also a summary of the outcome of completed trials.

This three-day workshop was hopefully helpful to my Mongolian colleagues. It was definitely a learning experience for me – in terms of realizing that even though Mongolians live in a very remote part of the world, they are informed about American issues – such as the debate about balancing our civil liberties with national security.

I think, however, that those Mongolians who do get a chance to visit the United States will be surprised to discover how unrealistically America is portrayed by Hollywood. Most of us don't drive around in expensive cars, live in mansions or wine and dine at expensive restaurants.

Perhaps most surprising to Mongolians would be the fact that there are places in America where cell phone just don't work – due to obstructions like buildings and mountains. In Mongolia, even in the farthest reaches, I usually got one or two bars on my mobile phone.

June 28, 2003

To the Steppe, Shamans and Reindeer People

The road from Ulaanbaatar to Khovsgul Lake reminds me of what it must have been like for the pioneers who traveled across the American west.

We left the asphalt some 100 kilometers from the capital. The rest of the 800-kilometer trip was on dusty trails. Most of the time we cruised across flat plains – passing yaks, goats, horses, cattle and sheep grazing nearby or sometimes in the middle of the track. Some of the lambs jumped to safety just seconds before we would slowly make our way through.

There were no fences – but the landscape was dotted with traditional Mongolian houses called gers – round structures covered with white canvas and lined with three or four layers of felt to keep out the 40-below-zero cold in winter. A stovepipe sticks out the center of the roof. In summer, the ger is nice and cool – and I found them to be a great place to take a nap after lunch.

Gers are ideal houses for nomads. They can be put up or taken down in less than an hour – and they can easily fit on a yak-drawn wagon.

We're bouncing along at 40-50 kilometers an hour in a new Toyota Land Cruiser. At times, our driver, Bataa, checks the on-board GPS unit to make sure we are on the right trail. Often, there are many paths to choose from across the grasslands – which are virtually surrounded by small mountains. We never really cross any mountains; we somehow manage to go around them.

Bataa often drives around the wooden bridges – uncertain whether they will support our weight. We notice a small herd of horses under one bridge – escaping from the mid-day summer heat. Grasshoppers are crackling through the grass around me as I take a short walk to stretch my legs.

Standing in a field of grass and wildflowers, the surrounding landscape reminds me of the American west -- at times I feel as though I'm in northern New Mexico, Arizona, Nevada and Utah. At one point, we spot a small lake. The shores are white and Bataa tells us it is salt.

We cross a small hill and spot a small runway – and a short time later the dirt road turns to asphalt. Suddenly, after hundreds of kilometers of bouncing about, the road is smooth and most welcoming.

We have arrived in Moron, pronounced just like the English word: moron.

I spent three days there.

Those days were spent conducting an assessment at two community radio stations to find out what their needs are. Both stations have two or three journalists. Everyone is under the age of 25. Only one reporter has had formal training at university.

Once I get an idea of what kinds of skills the journalists have and what they'd like to learn, I will design a training program specifically for them.

They're interested in learning the basics: developing story ideas, writing leads, conducting interviews and getting a deeper understanding of what exactly constitutes a news story.

Many have been doing community service announcements and calling that news. Each of the seven participants is thirsty for information and is pleased we have made the long journey to work with them.

The workshop is supposed to last four hours, but easily runs beyond five. We are meeting in a ger – and the roundness of the structure creates an atmosphere that is intimate. It is an ideal place to hold a workshop.

I leave with a sense that I have helped my fellow colleagues, but they've also helped me to understand what it's like to cover stories in a remote outpost in the middle of Mongolia. Most of them had had some basic journalism training and they were all enthusiastic about taking an idea and turning it into a story. I was particularly impressed with their topics: local corruption, the need to carry drinking water from long distances, the problem of rabid dogs in their town and how to develop the local tourism industry.

As I leave, I look forward to coming back. My colleagues seemed to genuinely enjoy the workshop and I felt we each learned something from this experience.

Our next stop is Khovsgol Lake – 100 kilometers north of Moron. It is Mongolia's top tourist destination. It's the second deepest lake in Central Asia and the water is so pure you can drink from it. (I did – and the water tasted sweet and cold). It is also so clear that you can see deep into its depths. I spotted a number of fish. The lake is surrounded by mountains – and ecologically, the area is part of Siberia. In winter, the lake freezes and trucks make their way across it on their way to and from Russia.

We have come to Khovsgol Lake to do a field workshop with Zaya – our translator. She also writes articles for a publication called Rural Business News and plans to produce a radio piece based on our interviews.

We arrive on July 4, just in time for two festivals that begin on the following two days. One is a shaman festival; the other is the reindeer festival.

At least three shamans have come to Khovsgul for a ritual in which they call on the spirits of their ancestors and spirits from nature to bless the people of the region. Two shamans, a frail looking elderly woman and a middle-aged woman, separately begin by slowly beating a drum and calling the spirits. Circles form around each woman – although an opening is left in each circle to allow spirits to come and go.

I am moved and fascinated by the ceremony – as it reminds me of a Native American ceremony with its chanting and drum beats. It is easy to fall into a hypnotic trance.

At times, the shamans begin to hiss – apparently to chase away any evil spirits. At other times, they sprinkle milk around them. This continues for nearly two hours. All the while, people are giving them cigarettes, water and vodka. The ritual concludes when each woman collapses from exhaustion or alcohol.

Shamanism was strongly discouraged during the Soviet years. While Mongolia was not an "official" Soviet republic, it was dominated by the USSR, and any practices that led people astray from Soviet doctrine were outlawed. Somehow, these old traditions have survived despite efforts to erase any trace of them.

The festival was started after the collapse of the Soviet Union.

The reindeer festival is more a gathering of reindeer herders with a few reindeer. Each summer, they bring their animals down from the mountains to the tall grass around Khovsgul Lake.

The reindeer people have traveled some 200 kilometers from their mountaintop homes. It took them three days on horseback – each bringing along some of their beautiful reindeer. They have set up camp in teepee-like shelters. One of the teepees stands out because it is covered with tree bark – and its owner tells me that it would last 20 years. In winter, the tree bark covering is replaced with reindeer hides.

One reindeer herder invites me to join him in his home – where I am served reindeer milk tea and curds. The curds are sliced into tiny blocks – and appear to have little flavor – until a short time after I swallow them – at which time there is an after-taste of salt.

The reindeer milk tea is served in a communal cup and is passed around starting with me. It's warm and tastes sweet, although it is hard to enjoy because there are so many flies trying to get a taste of it, too.

It's my first trip deep into the Mongolian countryside and it feels like I had stepped into a documentary film, particularly as I watched the shaman ceremony.

As I sat around the circle and the shamans chanted, I couldn't help but think about my own ancestors, who had had their own myths, rituals and ceremonies. But, we, as a society, have lost touch with many of these ancient traditions. It's a pity that we can only read about them, but here under the moon light and stars – an ancient people shared a living tradition that continues to be handed down from generation to generation. Somehow, it made me feel connected to my own ancestors and our own myths and legends.

Author's Note: Most of the road between Ulaanbaatar and Khovsgul Lake is still an unpaved dirt track.

Early July 2003

Stranger in the Night

The lock on my wooden ger in the western Mongolian city of Moron is busted, but it's a quiet, peaceful-like town and I figure: why bother.

I drift off to sleep only to be startled awake when the door of my ger creaks open and a young woman steps into the room. She flips on the light, sits on the edge of my bed and begins to speak to me in Mongolian. She is using hand gestures and picks up the book by my bed and gestures as if she is speed-reading – then slides her index finger down the middle of the page. What could it mean? Why is she here? She doesn't appear to be a prostitute.

She does appear to be getting frustrated now. So she gets up and goes over to my backpack and quickly scans the contents. She doesn't appear to be a thief – it's as if she is trying to find something that will help explain why she is here. The young woman then frantically looks across the room as if she is searching for something. All the while, I am lying in my single bed – watching – not sure what to make of it.

She comes back to sit on the edge of the bed and picks up the book again and makes the speed-reading gesture. I still don't get it. Maybe I should read to her in English?

After about 15 minutes she says two English words "I'm sorry" and gets up and walks out of the ger and into the night.

July 3, 2003

Naadam and Heartbreak

I can see the huge trail of dust miles off in the distance some 60 minutes before the riders start coming into view. My Mongolian friend exclaims excitedly, "It's them!" As the minutes tick by, the dust cloud slowly draws closer and closer – toward that magic spot just below me: the finish line.

Horseracing is one of three events during Naadam – the main summer festival in Mongolia that attracts virtually every Mongolian in the country. Mongolians who live abroad often schedule their visit home around Naadam. It is a big event celebrated since the time of Genghis Khan – the warrior who conquered much of the known world in the 12th century and is considered the founder of the Mongolian Empire.

Naadam comes from the word, naadah, which means "to play." When Mongolians play, they play hard.

The two other Naadam events are the manly sports of archery and wrestling.

The riders on horseback are between the ages of 7 and 12 – and their ride began at 12 noon – some 30 kilometers away from the finish line. Now, as it approaches 4 p.m. – a handful of riders emerge from the dust – maybe two minutes away from the finish.

The pounding hooves grow louder and the children on board seem to synchronize the rhythm of the tiny straps they use to strike the horses to keep them at full speed. Thirty seconds – the crowd begins to cheer – the music through the loudspeakers gets louder and more distorted. Ten seconds – a boy in a yellow outfit is the clear winner – riding maybe four seconds ahead of the next nearest rider. The youngster gallops off – and suddenly dozens of horses are crossing the finish line. It is an exhilarating moment for horse and rider – but also for the fans. I had never seen anything like it.

That moment is marred a short time later – because just 50 feet across the finish line – I notice a beautiful gray horse lying on the ground. People are gathering around it – trying to get the animal to get up. But it is too late – it dies moments after carrying its rider across the finish line.

A few moments later, I notice seven or eight people leading another horse around behind cars and trucks parked along the finish line. The animal is struggling to stand up and is being supported by the men and boys. The horse collapses – and they begin massaging and bending its legs – one man pours water on the animal's head – still another pounds on the animal's chest – attempting to restart its heart. The pounding goes on for more than a minute. The horse suddenly raises its head. The man continues to pound its chest.

Next, amazingly the animal gets back up. Its young rider is standing nearby – watching all this with curiosity. The horse's legs are wobbling, but the men keep massaging it. A few minutes later – the animal is led away.

These heartbreaking incidents leave an indelible mark on the day and on me.

I can't stop thinking about how these small, but powerful horses, had given their young riders every last bit of strength and endurance they had to carry them across the finish line.

July 11, 2003

Who's that Knocking

It started around midnight – a loud banging sound. Was someone moving a huge refrigerator down the steps outside my apartment? That's what it sounded like – thump, thump, thump – steel hitting concrete – hard.

Next came voices. Near, then far. A man, angry. A woman, upset. It continues for about half an hour – then quiet.

The following morning I am up early to catch a flight to Moron. I walk outside my apartment door and the steel door next to mine has been completed removed from the plaster wall; it is free-standing. Huge chunks of plaster lie on the landing. The inner door of the apartment is still intact, but the outer door is a wreck. The smell of plaster is heavy in the air. All is quiet at 6 a.m.

When I return one day later – the door has been reattached to the wall. The only remaining sign of the forced entry is new plaster around the door frame.

Perhaps they lost their keys.

July 16, 2003

Mutton in the Cargo Hold

The little lobby in the Moron airport was crowded with foreigners and Mongolians. Everyone was chatting – the atmosphere was friendly.

A woman approaches Zaya, my interpreter, and asked her to step over to the Mongolian Airline desk. When Zaya returns she has a baggage claim ticket and she points to a cardboard box over by the desk. "Freshly slaughtered mutton," she replies.

An elderly woman had asked Zaya if she would take the box back to UB for her relatives. Zaya readily agreed.

It's refreshing and makes me think of the innocence we once knew in the United States – when it was OK to help someone out by carrying a bag or a box onto a plane. That seems so long ago. There is no security check or metal detectors at this little airport in Moron. We simply walk out to the tarmac and climb the ladder and take our seats.

Zaya dutifully hands over the box of mutton upon arrival in Ulaanbaatar.

July 18, 2003

Cheap Seats

The flight back from Moron to UB is uneventful.

MIAT flight 55-72 leaves Moron 15 minutes early and the plane is full. It wasn't until we landed that I realized just how full.

I was sitting at the back of the plane and behind me was the bathroom and directly behind it was the cargo hold – separated from the main cabin by a cloth curtain. As I stood up and looked into the darkness of the cargo area – I saw eyes and began to hear voices. Looking more closely I begin to make out faces and bodies. At least ten people – maybe more – including at least one infant – had huddled atop suitcases in the cargo hold for the 80-minute flight from Moron.

I'm told the airfare is much cheaper than flying in coach, but the airline offers no snacks to those in the cargo hold.

Author's Note: *MIAT no longer flies domestically. The domestic routes are now flown by several private airlines that fly several types of planes, including the Airbus.*

July 18, 2003

Another Knock at the Door

There is pounding on my front door. I peep through the tiny hole in the door, but can't really tell who it is. The stairwell is too dark. I open the door.

A small man wearing black trousers, black leather shoes and a white shirt says the word "Iyun" – or so it sounds. I think he is asking for the woman who lived here before me. This had happened before and my colleagues had taught me what to say in Mongolian – so I said to him: "ter nussen," which literally translates to "she moved."

He is persistent – with an urgent look on his face.

I let him come in.

He removes his shoes and goes into the kitchen and points out the window. I now understand – the heavy rain is somehow getting into his apartment below mine from the roof outside my window.

I open the windows grab his shoes and help him climb out onto the roof. He twists the downspout away from the low place on the roof and builds a dam. Next, he crosses the roof and clears the gutter. The man washes his dirty hands in the water pouring from the downspout. I offer him a paper towel,he removes his shoes and climbs back in through the kitchen window.

The man shakes my hand, puts his shoes back on at the door and disappears down the dark stairs.

July 21, 2003

Oops. Sorry Mr. President

The soldier steps from the guard shack and moves quickly through the tall grass toward us – his Kalashnikov rifle swinging from his right shoulder. My friend, Ganaa, looks at me, grins and says, "We're in trouble."

As the soldier climbs onto the concrete road he asks why we are here. Ganaa replies, "We made a wrong turn on the ridge above us – and came off the mountain too soon." She apologizes.

The soldier escorts us to the main entrance. As we walk along, his rifle strap creaks as it swings against the metal hinge that holds the strap in place. It has a rhythm to it. The soldier begins to walk faster as we approach the guard station and the creaking sound grows faster.

Ganaa and I had just completed a six-hour hike – climbing a steep hillside to a ridge and then we had followed the ridge around to an evergreen forest and giant boulders. At times during the hike, there was no trail – and as we stepped through the high grass we could hear water gurgling beneath us. We parted the grass, dug into the soil and suddenly we saw the underground stream. We began to fill our water bottles. The water was icy cold and had a wonderfully sweet taste.

Now, the last of that water was jostles about in the bottle in my backpack as the armed soldier escorts us along a paved road toward a guard shack.

At the guard station by the main road – another soldier in a freshly pressed white shirt and pants asks for our identification. He then asks us to show him what's inside our backpacks. I'm a bit reluctant since I have a minidisc recorder and a professional microphone in the bag. I had been recording bird sounds in the mountains, but it might be interpreted as some sort of surveillance equipment.

Surprisingly, neither guard is interested in the electronic gear, but the one in the white pressed shirt begins dialing a number on one of three phones on his desk. He tells the person on the other end of the line about our situation, but that person apparently doesn't care and tells the guard to call someone else. The next person he calls didn't answer. Finally he reaches a third person who instructs him to write down our names.

All the while, a Mongolian soap opera is blaring on the 19-inch color television set on the guard's desk. He glances at the screen occasionally as he writes down our names. Finally, after 20 minutes, he returns our ID's and points us out the gate and back onto the main road.

Little did we know, we had wandered into the Prime Minister's summer compound.

July 26, 2003

Flesh and Fashion

It's not a good idea to drink too much when visiting the Marco Polo strip club. The wooden stairs are unbelievably steep and narrow. They remind me of the stairs leading into my grandmother's attic.

The Marco Polo is on the second or maybe it's the third floor of a building that houses an Italian eatery on the ground level. It's hard to tell which floor you're on because before climbing the wooden steps – one must ascend a series of steep winding marble steps with no hand-rail.

It's not your typical strip joint. Yes, the girls do take everything off, but for the most part they dance (with their clothes on) in a circle on a small stage. At times, there are 15 or so girls in this circle – showing off long gowns and bikinis. Some of them remove their clothing; others do not. It's more like a fashion show.

Suddenly, the so-called fashion show of dancing girls comes to an abrupt halt. The lights go down and in the darkness I can see movement. It's the main attraction arriving on stage -- a group of four female contortionists.

This is definitely unlike any strip club I have ever been to – anywhere.

These girls are amazing – and they keep their clothes on. After running onto the stage – they proceed to twist their bodies in every way imaginable and then some – to the beat of an Enigma tune. And they never miss a beat.

One minute they are entangled in their own spider web-like pose and the next they are stacked – back-to-stomach with their heads gazing out at the crowd of men – and women.

There are almost as many women in the club as there are men.

I'm there for a going-away party for a young Australian woman named Chris. She has spent the last eleven months in UB as editor of the English language weekly newspaper, the UB Post. Chris is moving to the UK to seek her fortune. Tonight, she has brought along some of her work mates – mostly Mongolian women – and three or four male friends.

Sitting next to me is Ruth – a young Irish woman who had literally just gotten off the plane from Tokyo not more than 90 minutes earlier. Her friend, Stevan, had picked her up at the airport, dropped her bags at his apartment and brought her straight to the restaurant and strip club.
Ruth isn't sure what to make of the whole thing.

We agree that we are probably contributing to the exploitation of women – but we also agree that this show is pretty tame compared to places like Bangkok. Our discussion is interrupted by a young Mongolian dancer who is dressed in a nearly see-through wedding gown. The gown has been cut into something like a two piece bikini – with a long skirt. She slowly makes her way toward me and begins dancing and moving erotically just inches from my face.

To my right sits Marie and her husband Bob. They have been to the Marco Polo once before and just now Bob is getting something close to a lap dance from leopard woman. This girl is dressed in a leopard skin bikini with matching leopard skin jacket and nearly knee-high boots. Bob slips one-thousand tugrug (one US dollar) into the leopard woman's right boot.

Marie doesn't seem uncomfortable with the whole thing. She watches and laughs as her husband sits back in his chair while the woman in the leopard skin bikini shakes her body in his face. He doesn't seem uncomfortable either. At times, he leans forward within a hairs' breath of touching the dancer. She has his undivided attention.

Stevan, who is seated across from me, is more interested in his mobile phone. As the girls dance around him he rarely looks up – preferring instead to keep his head buried in his electronic gadget – texting someone.

The girls don't seem to notice him, either, but he does attract the attention of the security guy. A young, burly Mongolian man comes up behind Stevan and stands over his left shoulder trying to figure out what he's doing with his phone. At one point, he taps Stevan on the shoulder and motions for him to leave. Stevan stands up – holds his little finger and thumb to his ear as if to explain to the guy that it's just a phone. The security man looks puzzled, but accepts Stevan's explanation; apparently having thought the device was a camera. Stevan resumes his text messaging.

Behind Stevan – along the wall – are a dozen or so Mongolian men – drinking beer and vodka and smoking cheap cigarettes. The dancers are particularly friendly to them and the guys seem to be a little too friendly with the girls.

The strippers rub their breasts and legs against the men – who in turn take the gesture as an invitation to touch the girls – in what would be considered inappropriate in most western strip clubs – where signs are usually posted that read, "Look, but don't touch."

The girls don't seem to mind being touched since most of the men are giving them big tips – sliding the tugrugs into the leather straps on their high heel shoes.

Later, just before midnight, Bob, his wife Marie and I slowly and carefully make our way down those steep, narrow steps and back out onto the streets of UB – above us – echoing from the Marco Polo Club we can hear strains of Tom Jones singing Sex Bomb.

Author's Note: *The Marco Polo Restaurant and Strip Club is still a part of the urban scape of Ulaanbaatar.*

July 31, 2003

To Ride

The freedom one feels on the back of a galloping horse on an open range surrounded by mountains and a winding river is almost indescribable. Nothing else exists at that moment except you and your horse. You feel the power of the horse as it dashes across the plain – its massive muscles working in rhythm as you search for that same rhythm to become one with the beast. There are few things more exciting to me than being able to find that oneness and just go with it – loosen the reins and let my horse and me be free.

I have just such an experience during a ride in the Terejl National Preserve about 80 or so kilometers northeast of UB. The landscape is dramatic. Huge boulders and massive rock piles left over from the Ice Age dot the landscape. They eventually give way to beautiful plains that are divided by a river that snakes through the grassland.

As any rider knows, the moment you swing your leg across the saddle – your horse is evaluating you. It's determining whether you are nervous, somewhat confident or totally in control. The horse then reacts to you.

I must have given my horse the wrong impression. It refuses to do anything except walk. I am lucky if it breaks into a trot – a gallop seems out of the question.

I notice that my friend Ganaa (most Mongolians used only a single name) is thoroughly enjoying herself. She has a fast horse that has a beautiful gallop. Ganaa is a natural on horseback. She rides comfortably and with lots of confidence.

It wasn't always that way. She told me that she had fallen from horses on four different occasions, but she always climbed back on. Now, watching her lean her body toward the horse's mane – Ganaa looks like she had been born on a horse.

Admittedly, I am a little envious and Ganaa notices because she gallops up beside me and offers me her horse. At first, I refuse, but then accept. We trade saddles and horses and I swing my leg across the saddle.

I can feel the energy in this horse. It's anxious to move.

I click my tongue against the roof of my mouth and the horse takes off. We gallop along a narrow trail through the woods and come to a river about four feet deep. I pull my feet and legs up against the horse's belly to stay dry and slowly cross the water.

Once on the river bank there is nothing but open grassland and a few gers in front of me. I click my tongue against the roof of my mouth again and the horse bolts across the long field. Herds of cows, goats and sheep are to my right – the river 100 yards to my left and mountains off in the distance in all directions.

I lean into the wind, hold the reins loose, push my knees into the sides of the horse and find the horse's rhythm within my own body. As the horse pushes forward, I push forward. I feel my body bouncing slightly – as if keeping a rhythm not just with the horse's body, but also with the horse's hooves as they pound the earth.

I feel exhilaration and timelessness.

The warm sun, the dark blue sky, the light breeze in my face, the sense of freedom and stillness and the beautiful landscape: What more could I want?

August 2, 2003

Flat Tires and Bad Beds

My driver, Batsaikhan, and I grin at each other, as we each put our hands together under our chins in Buddhist fashion and bow – praying to the road gods. I initiated this impromptu prayer and afterward, we both look at each other and laugh, nervously.

We are still 80 or so kilometers from our destination – Baruur-Urt -- in Sukhbaatar Aimag (province) in eastern Mongolia – and we have no more spare tires.

In the last 40 kilometers we punctured both back tires on our Toyota Land Cruiser. If we lose another one – we're camping in the grasslands. Not such a bad idea, really. After all, it's early autumn and not so cold at night.

As we cruise along on some of the worst dirt roads I've experienced in Mongolia -- I'm quietly fantasizing about sleeping under the starry skies and a half-moon – with all the night critters -- in the middle of nowhere.

We had driven all day – coming from Ulaanbaatar -- some 600 kilometers. For lunch, we stopped at a canteen with a covered area outside with benches. Batsaikhan, my translator, Zaya and I grabbed a table. The waitress immediately brought us milk tea and took our orders. We each ordered Tsuivan – a traditional Mongolian dish of noodles, carrots, chunks of mutton and fat.

As we waited for our food, a Russian minivan (regional transportation) pulled up – packed with people. Each person clambored out – climbing over gasoline cans and the legs of other passengers. Some people huddled together – having packed their own lunches. The rest scrambled into the canteen. Tsuivan appeared to be the most popular dish. Everyone was ordering it. There's usually no menu at these canteens; it's the cook's choice.

After nearly 40 minutes our food arrived. Zaya and I sprinkled red hot pepper over ours – and I carefully picked around the chunks of mutton fat. Tsuivan is becoming my favorite dish on the road; sometimes it's the only dish! And it's quite tasty – particularly when you've been bouncing around on dirt roads all day.

Back on the road, the landscape is breathtaking. The sky is as blue as a Georgia O'Keefe landscape – and the puffy clouds are hanging in layers just above the horizon. At times, the green hillsides seem to touch the sky – and it's as if the hilltop is the edge of the Earth – and if you climbed to the top – you'd just fall off.

Toward day's end, we make a wrong turn and wind up driving through a field of tall grass for almost an hour. But – the side trip is a stroke of pure luck. We spot plenty of wildlife: dozens of gazelles, a couple of small foxes, a dozen or so falcon, marmots and domesticated camels.

It was toward sunset – as we were listening to an Abba song on the cassette player – that we had our first blowout. As we replaced the tire – the sky behind us turned shades of yellow, orange and purple. Before this sunset show was over – we were back on the dirt road – cruising at 60 kilometers an hour.

I mention that we were listening to Abba only because it was in the middle of Abba's Fernando that we experienced our second blowout – a result of very sharp rocks on the road – or was it the Abba music? It was only after this tire change that we began to wonder if we'd make Baruur-Urt – and I'd be able to start my journalism workshop the following morning.

As we make our way – there is a signpost – every three kilometers
-- ticking down the mileage: 21 – then 18 – and finally at three kilometers
– we see the lights of Baruur-Urt. We slowly make our way into town
and find our hotel – the only hotel in town.

The bed is worn out – the springs sticking up randomly through
the mattress -- but the sheets are clean. The TV sits in the corner, but
there is no outlet to plug it into. The toilet keeps gurgling and hissing –
and the tap water – hmmm. I turn the cold water faucet on, but it only
spits a few drops of water. It's just enough to wash the smell of sardines
off my fingers. Forget about any hot water. This hotel room is billed as
only half-luxury – which translates to dripping water, bad bed springs
and no TV.

Author's Note: *The road between Ulaanbaatar and Baruur Urt*
is now a two-lane paved road.

August 6, 2003

Baruur Urt

The sound of hooves pounding the concrete breaks the momentary silence on the street below. Horses pulling wooden carts share the main street of Baruur Urt with Russian jeeps and minibuses, motorcycles, the occasional rider on horseback and the cattle that wander about picking grass on the edge of the road.

The street is surprisingly busy for a small town with a population of just over 10,000 residents. It's the town where revolutionary hero Sukhbaatar was born. He was a Mongolian military figure who led the drive for Mongolia's independence during the revolution of 1921 that ultimately saw the communists sweep into power. Sukhbaatar sits atop his horse at the monument on the small square in front of governor's house in Baruur Urt.

This main government building happens to house the best restaurant in town. The goulash is delicious. It consists of tender chunks of roast beef with rice, shredded carrots and cole slaw on the side.

Our host, Munkhbat, who is the manager of FM 102.5, also orders potato salad for everyone. I have had potato salad in the countryside about three times before – but this particular dish is the tastiest yet. Potato salad, a Russian dish, became popular in Mongolia during the Soviet years.

Behind governor house is the market area – or as the locals call it – the black market – a name that is also a holdover from Soviet times. When residents didn't want to wait in long lines, they headed to the black market – and paid a bit more for fruits and vegetables.

There are dozens of stalls – with vendors selling all sorts of produce and household goods. Today, there happens to be sack upon sack of onions stacked outside the booths. Further down, the red ripe tomatoes look tasty, but it is the freshly baked loaves of bread that catch my eye – and I buy a loaf from an elderly woman for about 25 US cents.

I had no idea when I was buying the bread that on Friday afternoons – all the restaurants and liquor stores shut down for the day. Later that evening, back at the hotel, which is the only one in town, my driver, Batsaikhan, Zaya, my translator and I fix a delicious meal. Sitting under a dim light bulb dangling from the ceiling of my room, we make the bread the centerpiece of our feast. We top it with fresh cheese and sardines – and use my Swiss Army knife to spear the scrumptious and crunchy German pickles.

Hanging on the wall behind the little dinner table is an embroidered rug with Genghis Khan – sitting on a throne – looking very fatherly. The rug covers soiled wallpaper that looks like it was put up when the hotel went up in the early 1980's. The bathroom too has been seriously neglected. The toilet has a mind of its own – randomly burping at all hours. It is, however, the one thing that works in the bathroom. There is a huge tub, but the water from the faucets only drips occasionally. The light bulb hanging from the high ceiling constantly flickers.

The staff is attentive. I have no working electrical plugs for my computer and mobile phone, but the hotel staff fixes the problem quickly by running a wire along the edge of the wall and attaching an outlet to the end of it. Shockingly, it works!

Outside, dogs are constantly barking through the night – and Russian jeeps and trucks roar down the concrete street at all hours – their engines echoing off the walls of the buildings. Most of the vehicles appear to be heading west toward Ulaanbaatar – perhaps coming from the Chinese border – just 80 kilometers from Baruur Urt.

One is instantly reminded of just how close that border is simply by turning on the radio. There is only one FM station in Baruur Urt – and it signs off at 8 p.m. each night. On the AM band, there are no Mongolian stations, but the airwaves are jammed with Chinese stations, particularly at night.

Tonight, the Chinese music competes with those barking dogs. Not too far in the distance, the flapping of a punctured truck tire and the rustling of leaves from the trees just outside my balcony window are the last sounds I hear before drifting off to sleep.

August 9, 2003

Mistaken Identity?

I am climbing the front steps to my friend, Jim's, hotel when suddenly a woman shouts from the sidewalk, "Excuse me, excuse me." I look around – expecting to see someone I know. She is unfamiliar – wearing a black dress and designer glasses. She is Mongolian.

At first, I assume she knows Jim – who is walking through the front door ahead of me. I glance at him, but he looks back at me with a totally blank expression on his face.

The woman is focused on me. She is out of breath and frantically speaking German. I know that it is German because my friend Ganaa, who is standing beside me, speaks German as well. Ganaa tells the woman that I am not German, but American. The woman ignores her – telling me in German that she has been following me for blocks – that she thought she recognized me. She says, "I thought you were a doctor." She then declares, "You're the German doctor who performs kidney transplants."

The woman continues to insist that I am German. She grabs my arm and tugs at me – urging me to go with her. In German, she says, "Come with me, come with me."

I am genuinely curious about what it is she wants, but, of course, I have no intention of following her. Is she drunk? I don't smell alcohol on her breath. Her appearance is quite normal – except that she is still frantically speaking German to me – ignoring my friends – and demanding that I go with her.

Finally, she steps back – gives me one final look – and walks down the steps, up the sidewalk and around the corner out of sight.

Mosquitoes

Sometimes, I am a light sleeper. Several times, since moving to Ulaanbaatar I have been awakened from light sleep by a single mosquito buzzing about my ear.

Mosquitoes in Mongolia? I never expected it. But they are plentiful during the short Mongolian summer.

I have been buzzed often.

Strangely, I never see them by day. It is only in the middle of the night that they seem to appear. Actually, I rarely see them – I'm aware they're around because of that signature buzzing sound they make.

I swat at them – and lie awake – waiting for their return. But they seem to sense when I have fallen back to sleep. The next morning, I have bites on my neck, hands and arms.

By late August, I expected the cold nights would have taken care of those pesky little biters, but they don't seem to mind the cool. Last night, for the first time in weeks, I was buzzed. At first, I thought I was hearing a distant siren. But I kept listening – hard. Sure enough, the sound got a little louder. Mosquito. And this little guy was persistent – no matter how much I swatted he kept returning. First, it was my left ear – then he moved to my right. Buzzzzzzzzzzzz.

I covered my entire body and head with the sheet and blanket – and fell back to sleep to the sound of a siren – far, far off in the distance.

August 25th, 2003

In Search of the Mother Stone

The rolling fields of grass soon give way to fields of oddly shaped boulders. Some of them look like totem poles with naturally carved faces – others, far in the distance, appear to be buildings. As we bounce along on the vast Mongolian steppe in an SUV, I imagine they are the tops of skyscrapers.

Are these stones the children of the Eej Khad or Mother Rock? The Mother Rock is a naturally formed rock formation that is considered sacred by Mongolians.

As our vehicle slowly ascends the hillsides, it feels like we will drop off the Earth as we approach the top. All that we can see is an ultramarine sky directly in front of us. It looks so close it's almost like we can reach out and touch it. I half expect to cross the hillside and there will be the vast Mother Rock – something so vast that it will leave me in awe.

We drive for more than two hours on little more than cow trails. Our driver speaks no English, so we can't ask him how far. It's not something you do in Mongolia anyway. Never ask the driver how much longer it will take. They believe it will jinx the trip and something terrible will happen.

So we keep bouncing along – dodging giant boulders and the occasional cow, yak and horse. We are miles from civilization. Actually, we are just 15 kilometers from a village, but it seems farther when you aren't driving on roads.

Suddenly we cross the top of a hill and see three or four gers, a couple dozen people, two or three dogs, half a dozen cars and a parking sign.

As our driver pulls into a spot, I gesture, "Where's the Mother Rock?" He points to a round, wooden ger. My girlfriend, Robyn, looks back at me as if to say: "We drove 100 kilometers of bad road for this?"

I had purposely not read up on Mother Rock. I enjoy the sense of adventure and surprise. And this is definitely turning out to be a surprise. I quickly comment: "Well, let's see what it's all about."

We climb from the SUV and make our way across a trash-strewn parking area and into the huge ger – which has a diameter of about 40 feet. I can smell boiled mutton as I cross the threshold. Directly in front of me is a giant stone that stands about eight feet high. It looks like a very overweight human. It's wrapped in golden cloth and blue Buddhist ribbons hang from the shoulders of this boulder.

A man on crutches is bending over the stone – placing his head upon what would have been the chest area. He holds his head there for maybe 30 seconds – then moves counter clockwise around to the right shoulder and leans against the stone. He then hobbles over to the other side and does the same thing. As he makes his way around the stone – other pilgrims move counter clockwise around the inner perimeter of the ger – at the back, behind the Mother Rock – is an altar – covered with half-empty vodka bottles. Incense is burning on the altar – giving the glass bottles a sparkling glow.

Our driver makes his own pilgrimage – placing his head against the Mother Rock – his lips moving – as he recites what appears to be a silent prayer.

He may be asking the Mother Rock for advice. Few foreign tourists come here – one of the reasons I wanted to visit – but plenty of Mongolians make the trip – seeking the solitude and advice from this sacred stone. Many believe the stone has the power to fulfill their prayers.

This trip had been a surprise – a pleasant one that at first admittedly seemed like a giant waste of time. I'm glad that I spent some time at Mother Rock, but I can't say I felt any special powers emanating from the stone.

Yet what was most fulfilling to me was taking in the peaceful surroundings and watching the steady stream of Mongolians place their heads, hearts and hopes upon the stone.

September 4, 2003

The Train to Beijing

I awake in the middle of the night to the sound of the wind blowing across the train car. It's a desolate sound – in what looks like a desolate place.

Out the window and through the darkness, I can make out a grassy plain stretching for miles. The nearly full moon gives the landscape a yellow eeriness – the wind continues to whistle through the slight opening in my carriage window.

Why has the train stopped here? There are no sidetracks for another train to pass. Occasionally, in the distance, I can hear steel striking steel – a slight sound that makes for an even more surreal feeling. There are no other sounds.

I have been on the train from Ulaanbaatar to Beijing for 17 hours – another 14 and I will arrive in the Chinese capital.

It has been a bit of a strange evening.

Four hours earlier at the border, I was taken off the train for nearly an hour – where Mongolian Customs agents scrutinized my passport and visa – which they had confiscated 90 minutes earlier.

I was more curious than nervous about the whole thing. An agent escorted me from the train to a building near the tracks. I was brought into a room with more than a half dozen desks – the young woman who had asked me to step off the train then opened a small case with a combination lock and removed my passport.

49

Two Pakistani men had also been taken from the train along with me. They spoke broken English and I helped them communicate with the Customs agent.

The chief agent eventually motioned for me and one of the Pakistani men to leave the room. He gestured for us to sit outside, but there were no seats. We stood outside the door – looking at each other.

Eventually, my two new friends were escorted back to the train. I then stood alone outside the doorway – waiting and wondering why there was a problem. I had been keeping an eye on my train – just outside, but this time when I looked out – I couldn't see it. For an instant, I wondered if I had been left behind, but looking more closely I saw the faint lights of the train just beyond the platform.

A tall man with a pressed uniform soon arrived and the young woman, who had escorted me off the train began to point at the visa page of my passport – uncertain how to proceed.

I knew that my visa was in order, but perhaps these customs agents had gotten confused. My entry date to Mongolia had been June 16, but my visa entry said June 27. Still, there should not have been a problem since Americans don't need a visa for a visit of less than three months. My visa was a multi-entry one that was good until May of the following year. Maybe these guys were just bored in the middle of the night and needed something to break this boredom.

After another 20 minutes, I am asked to sign a document that is written in Mongolian at which time my passport was returned to me and the young woman pointed toward the door.

As I walked back to the train in the crisp night air – a soldier gestured toward my carriage. Yes, my train was still there. Another soldier asks for my passport – glances at it and motions for me to climb back aboard.

Seconds later, the train pulls out of the station bound for Beijing.

Had I been frightened by this ordeal? No, not really – and I can't say why. Perhaps it was because I felt confident the Mongolian customs agents would work it out and I would be on my way. Then, too, there was this whole sense of adventure. Honestly, I was more curious than anxious.

September 11, 2003

Autumn in Ulaanbaatar

The mountains east of Ulaanbaatar appear to be on fire as the sun rises over them. The whole mountainside is glowing, fiery red – as if a volcano is erupting just behind it.

My yellow taxi is driving straight toward this apocalyptic-like scene, but the driver hardly notices as he tunes his radio to a Mongolian pop music station. Outside the car window – the sky is still quite dark and gray clouds are hovering low overhead. Despite the low clouds, one still gets a sense of wide open space because the horizon seems endless.

Due west – on the opposite mountain, a few rays of sunlight are turning the birch tree leaves a spectacular bright yellow. The larch pines are shedding their needles and the morning sun turns them a mustard color. Slowly, the shadows on the mountain give way to brilliant reds, blues and greens – those vibrant greens come from the huge evergreen forest. The evergreen needles and yellow birch leaves and larch pine needles complement each other perfectly. I am momentarily transported to the Colorado Rockies.

The arrival of autumn in Mongolia reminds me of fall in the Rockies – except there is a much greater sense of urgency here. Building crews are working faster - trying to complete construction projects before the frigid winter puts everything on hold; the fruit and vegetable stands now have freshly harvested apples, turnips and cabbage; stores are starting to stock horse meat on their shelves - Mongolians say this meat keeps the body warmer than other meats. They make horse buuz – a large steamed dumpling of horse meat and garlic.

As I step outside each morning, I can smell the crisp, yellow leaves as they give off an earthy, decaying scent. The air has a chill to it, the darkness lingers a bit longer and the people on the street are already beginning to bundle up and walk a bit faster.

Another sign of autumn -- the radiators in the apartments and offices are beginning to get warm – helping to knock off that early morning chill.

The flowers – black eyed susans, marigolds and the grayish-white edelweiss -- continue to brave this cooler air. I can't help but wonder when the first real cold snap will arrive – the so-called killing frost. So far, 8 degrees Celsius has been the lowest temperature I have experienced in Mongolia, but I am told to expect 35 degrees below zero – in the dead of winter.

September 25, 2003

Way out West in Bayan Olgii

When we arrived at the airport in Bayan Olgii, we had no idea where we would sleep – much less whether or not we'd have a bed. We had only been assured that we would not have to sleep outside. That was comforting in that temperatures in October in far western Mongolia drop into the low single digits.

After stepping off the ancient Soviet-built prop plane, we are greeted by a local freelance journalist who assures us we will have a hotel room. Rooms are hard to find because of the annual Eagle Hunting festival this weekend. Tourists, both Mongolians and foreigners, have booked virtually everything – and there are only about four hotels in the whole town.

My co-worker Bayar, my translator Ganaa and I soon arrive in the center of Olgii – and pull up in front of a bar called Otau or Blue. We are told it has rooms.

It is your typical countryside Mongolian hotel.

It has a disco/bar/restaurant with Mongolian pop tunes blaring from a cheap boom box, peeling paint on the walls, dark hallways and stairways with a single low-watt bulb hanging from the ceiling. The bathrooms are filthy and there is no hot water. There is also no heat. OK, there is a little bit of heat if you sit on top of the lukewarm radiators.

Bayan Olgii is majority Muslim and ethnic Kazakh while the rest of Mongolia is Tibetan Buddhist. Mongolians who'd traveled to this province had said it was, for them, like traveling to another country because of the cultural and religious differences. Within an hour of our arrival, we are reminded of the religious differences as loudspeakers atop the mosques begin announcing the call to prayer.

As we walk around the town, we spot the largest of the six mosques in Bayan Olgii – a small building with a dome and several crescents on small shafts affixed to the minarets. The mosque is tucked away on a back street with a small fenced garden and walkway leading to the entrance. A few days later, the director of the mosque gave me a personal tour.

A short walk from the mosque is the town's outdoor market. The market has narrow dirt alleyways with vendors selling fruits and vegetables, cheap clothing, shoes, toys, traditional Kazakh wall hangings and tortsogs – small, colorful, round domed hats worn by Muslims. Most of the tortsogs are black with bright designs stitched onto them.

Kanu, the editor of the local radio station, wears one with bright green stitching.

Our first evening in Bayan Olgii, Kanu takes us to a talent show at the local auditorium.

The theater is packed – mainly young people – who have come to cheer on their friends from the three western Aimags (provinces) – competing in what Kanu describes as the young people's festival. Many of the teenagers wave giant flags. We find three seats on the front row and settle in for the night's entertainment.

Most of the contestants sing pop tunes to distorted recorded music that blasts from the loudspeakers. Some of the talent has potential. One young woman in particular has a beautiful voice and fortunately the recorded pop music is not too distorted as she performs her song. She plays well to the audience and seems to be extremely comfortable on the stage.

Another young woman dressed in traditional Kazakh clothing walks onto the stage with a two-stringed instrument and begins to play. She is rather tall and she looks like she will have a powerful deep voice. The audience appears startled when she starts to sing. The woman has an amazingly hi-pitched voice. I think the four judges are caught by surprise, too. Out of a possible five points – each of them give her 2's and 3's.

The auditorium is one of the tallest buildings in Bayan Olgii. Made of brick, it is the centerpiece of the town. But a 7.5 earthquake three days earlier has left its mark on the building. Across the front wall inside the auditorium there is a two to three inch crack. Huge chunks of plaster have fallen into the seats. I am somewhat reluctant to remain inside the theater, but Kanu assures us that structural engineers have pronounced the building as sound.

Afterward, as we walk across the dusty road to our hotel, I glance westward; the moonlight illuminates the year-round snowcapped peaks – giving them a yellowish glow. High overhead, a million stars have come out. The chilly, mountain air stings my face, but I stop for several minutes to look for familiar constellations. To the southeast I spot a red dot; is it Mars rising fast in the Mongolian sky?

October 6, 2003

The Eagle Festival

I spot my first golden eagle in Bayan Olgii the morning of the start of the annual Eagle Festival. Actually, I see five golden eagles. They are resting on the arms of their owners – ethnic Kazakhs – who rode into town on horseback and are now sitting atop their horses and chatting with friends in the town's main square. Bayan Olgii is the only largely Kazakh populated Mongolian province.

The festival was started in 2000 by a local eagle hunter's association with support from a U.S.-based tourism company. The event has continued to grow each year.

The birds are stunning – and I find myself staring at these creatures – having never seen them this close up before. The feathers around their heads are slightly yellow – their heads are perfectly chiseled – handsome creatures with piercing eyes. Their claws are huge, sharp and deadly to their prey. One bird suddenly stretches – it has a wingspan of more than six feet.

This little performance is just a sampling of what is to come later outside town at the festival site.

Our group of reporters, all Mongolian except for me, jump into a Russian minivan and head east – about 15 kilometers out of Bayan Olgii. As we drive, we see dozens of older people walking toward the festival. None ask for a ride – it is part of a competition to see who will arrive at the site first.

The winner is a 75-year old man who allows me to snap his picture. But first, he wants to put on his jacket. The front of his jacket is covered with dozens of military medals – including one for his bravery in the 1939 war between Mongolia and Japan. On his head, he wears a bright orange tortsog made of black felt. As he stands proudly for the photograph, the man tells my translator that he will definitely compete in next year's walking competition.

Around us are literally dozens of eagle hunters on horseback with their birds sitting prominently on their forearms. Some hunters have slipped leather blinds over the birds' heads to cover their eyes to help keep them stay calm until the competition. Some of the eagles make high-pitched shrieks as they quickly turn their heads 360 degrees. One eagle chirps constantly – and its owner tells me that when eagles are taken from the nest at a very young age – they chirp for their mothers for about one year. This particular bird is competing at the festival for the first time.

Further on, I meet the oldest hunter in the competition, an 85-year-man who wears huge prescription sunglasses, a traditional Kazakh fox fur-lined red cap and at least six layers of clothing – the outermost being a traditional Kazak overcoat called a chapan. He tells me that he has three sons competing in the festival and that he has trained 30 eagles over the past 62 years.

The festival is held on an open plain with a small hillside toward the west. The first of the two-day competition begins with a parade. First the 65 eagle hunter's ride in pairs in a huge circle – their horses walking the first time around, next they trot and finally they do a full gallop with dust rising all around them. It feels like I have stepped into an old Western movie.

The competition begins with each hunter climbing half way up the hillside into the rocks – where he hands his eagle to a man – who then holds the bird while the hunter rides about 30 yards back down into the flats.

At this point, the man releases the bird and the hunter begins calling his bird. These few seconds are what the 400 or so tourists have come to see. In many cases, the eagles fly down the hillside – and make a beeline for their owners – landing perfectly on their forearms. Not an easy maneuver for either the hunter or the bird – because the horse is moving at a full gallop – and the hunter is trying to guide his horse, keep an eye on his eagle and call it – all at the same time. Once the bird lands – the hunter must maintain his balance – which can also be difficult because the bird weighs – on average – about 20 kilograms.

Some of the eagles take advantage of this moment of freedom and ignore their owners – choosing instead to soar around the hillside. They don't usually go very far though. Their feet are tied together and as a result most of the birds land in the rocks and sit and watch as their owners climb off their horses and stumble up into the rocks and grab the birds.

There is no shortage of food at the festival; everyone brings a picnic lunch and spreads a cloth onto the rocky ground. I am invited to join a group of people who have brought along a feast of breads, meats, biscuits, soda and, of course, vodka. A glass of vodka is passed around – with each person either passing, sipping or gulping it.

Cars, jeeps and minivans are parked haphazardly about – inside some of them are wolves and foxes. One man has two wolves chained inside the back of his pickup truck. They begin to growl as he climbs into the bed. Their teeth are a pearly white and very sharp. Their eyes have wildness about them – nothing like dogs' eyes.

Another man has a baby wolf on a leash and is walking around the festival grounds – at times the wolf tugs violently against the silver log chain – demanding to go its own way, but the man firmly jerks the chain and the wolf obeys. The man tells me it is almost a year old.

Still another man is carrying a beautiful fox with long reddish hair. It is gentle and he allows the children to pet it. The fox has a long nose and cunning-looking eyes. Traditionally, the fox is one of the favorite preys of the eagle, but today this fox is just for show.

The last event of the day doesn't involve eagles.

Judges are tossing four sets of plastic flowers onto the ground. Young riders on horseback must move at top speed, bend over and touch the flowers. It requires very good balance and most riders make it look easy. Just one rider actually tumbles off his horse.

Promptly at 5 p.m. the competition ends and we climb back into our Russian minivan and make our way back to town. Some in our group begin to sing a song about mother – and suddenly everyone is singing.

The next song is about a bird – and the male voices harmonize beautifully with the four females. Next is a Russian tune, Moscow Nights, and then another song about mother. I like this idea of spontaneous singing. It's something that we have lost in America, but here it just seems natural.

As we bounce along on the gravel road – our van no doubt carries some of the happiest people in all of Bayan Olgii. We continue our songs – both Mongolian and American – back at our hotel – drinking vodka – and chasing it with biscuits, 7-Up and bottled water.

Next day, the second day of the Eagle Festival, begins with a dusty ride into the countryside inside a Lada – an eight-year-old white Russian sedan. As we drive along a dirt track the dozen or so kilometers outside Olgii, dust pours in from every hole and every air vent in the car. At one point, the driver attempts to close the vents, but his efforts are in vain. Even the Kermit the Frog gear knob is covered with dust as we pull up to the festival site.

As we climb out of the car and dust ourselves off, the eagle hunters are on horseback taking turns pulling a piece of rabbit or fox fur behind them. On the hilltop above, their eagles are being released and most of the eagles swoop down and grab the fur. One of the fastest birds zeroes in on its "prey" within fifteen seconds after being released. Several eagles ignore their masters and instead decide to enjoy their moment of freedom and check out the hillside. Several eagle hunters tell me that there are too many people and that the temperature is too warm – that eagles prefer to hunt in colder weather.

October 5, 2003

My host, Shinai, a kindly man, knows virtually every eagle hunter in the competition and introduces me to many of them. Shinai is the reporter for Mongol Radio and also one of the organizers.

At one point during the day, he comes up to me and tells me that he wants to introduce me to an eagle hunter and his two sons – who are also taking part in the festival with their own eagles.

The next thing I know the man, called Mana, has taken off his chapan – a traditional Kazakh coat and his traditional fox fur hat and put them on me. I gladly hand over my down-filled jacket and AP Radio cap – which he puts on.

Next, Mana points toward his prized horse and motions for me to climb aboard. Mana then hands me his eagle and protective glove. Within a few seconds I am transformed into a Kazakh eagle hunter and I'm attracting a huge crowd – mainly tourists and a Japanese film crew, but also fellow eagle hunters who surround me with their horses and begin to grin and welcome me into their group.

It is one of those moments that I will never forget – particularly when Mana tells me to go have some fun on his horse. After returning his 20 kilogram eagle, I climb onto his horse, click my tongue and the animal starts trotting. I have never seen a horse trot in such a precise and dainty manner. It's an incredibly smooth ride. Later, Shinai tells me Mana has trained the horse to trot this way – and that not all horses can do it.

I try galloping Mana's horse, but the wooden saddle proves too painful – so I let my four-legged friend do his perfect little trot.

Mana has also brought a young wolf to the festival and he tells me that later that afternoon he will release it and let the eagles attempt to capture it. I wonder if they'll be allowed to kill it. Mana won't say. He urges me to wait and watch.

Just after the sun goes behind the hilltop, one of his sons brings out the wolf. It looks frightened and very shy. I'm not sure I want to watch. I am afraid the eagles will gang up and kill it.

The wolf is dragged to the middle of the field – and released. About that time, one eagle is released and the wolf starts to run toward the nearby rocky hillside. Before the wolf has gone ten yards, the eagle pounces on its back – suddenly another eagle appears and the two birds and the wolf are rolling in the rocks and bushes. Then, the wolf breaks free and a cheer goes up among the crowd of 200 or so who are watching from the sidelines. But then, several more hunters release their eagles and suddenly six or so birds re-capture the wolf as it fights back furiously. Several eagle hunters run out to the wolf and appear to hold it down as the eagles repeatedly pounce on their prey. Moments later, it is all over.

I spot Mana in the group of eagle hunters and he is placing a chain around his wolf's neck and leads it away. Amazingly, the wolf appears untouched.

The next day at lunch, Mana tells me that his wolf suffered a minor scratch on its back from a stone when it was attacked by the eagles. And he assures me he had no intention of letting his wolf get killed – not yet anyway. Mana says he wants to raise the wolf to adulthood – at which point he tells me matter-of-factly that he might kill it for its hide.

His comment troubles me deeply, but I try not to betray any feeling as he tells me his plans. His life is very different from mine – he has his own values and his own culture. To him, raising the wolf and then possibly killing it is the most natural thing to do. The animal hide will serve a purpose – a need. It will not be wasted.

The Eagle Festival minus the Eagles

Late in the afternoon of the second day of the festival, a huge crowd gathers around a square area marked off with rocks to watch the nukbar competition. It consists of two riders on horseback and a white goatskin. The referee walks into the square and tosses the goatskin into the air. After it hits the ground one rider attempts to approach the skin – and reaches down from his saddle and picks it up. It's not very easy to do for two reasons. Physically, it is difficult for the rider to almost touch the ground from the saddle. Psychologically it's not easy for the horse. Many horses get spooked around white objects by their feet.

After one rider grabs the goatskin, he has a few seconds to wrap one end tightly around his arm. The other rider then grabs the other end and it becomes a tug of war. The crowd roars as the riders almost slip from their saddles as they pull desperately on the goatskin until finally one of them grabs it and rides proudly around the marked off area before tossing the skin back on the ground.

The competition goes on for about two hours and at times the competitive edge gets so intense the riders move out of the square – where upon the crowd quickly disperses – getting out of the way of the horses.

Occasionally, fights break out among the competitors – usually because one of the riders thinks the other has cheated. At one point, police handcuff two people and take them away in a Russian jeep.

Nukbar reminds me of bushkazi, a violent game also played on horseback in Central Asia – with riders attempting to wrestle a goat or sheep carcass from other riders. It's played in a much larger space – usually the size of one or two soccer fields.

Shinai had been telling me all afternoon that the final event of the day was not on the schedule. It didn't actually happen, but would have been fun to watch. He said it involved an unmarried girl and boy. They would each climb onto horses and the boy would take off at a gallop. A few seconds later, the girl would chase after him and if she caught him – she could touch him with her horsewhip. It was supposed to be a sign of true love.

Unfortunately, at the end of the day, the single girls and boys climbed onto Russian motorbikes with sidecars and took off across the Mongolian plain.

Author's Note: The Eagle Festival is still held in Bayan Olgii each autumn with a second one each spring about one hour from Ulaanbaatar at the Terelj National Preserve.

Monoliths, Mounds and Horsemeat

The blue Russian jeep bounces around the dry, rocky riverbed at 40 kilometers an hour as we head out of Olgii. Our destination: a stone monolith and burial mound and if there's time, we might just do a little fishing.

The temperature hovers around minus 5 degrees Celsius, but our jeep has a heater and the driver keeps it humming.

As we drive through a rocky plain, suddenly off in the distance we see the monolith – standing about ten feet high and two feet square. Flat stones surround it – and on one stone is a roughly chiseled circle – nearly identical to one on the monolith itself. These "stamps" are thought to have belonged to a tribe called "Hongirad" – which had been around since before the time of Genghis Khan in the 12th century. It may have been the "Hongirad" who placed the stone monolith on this flat plain some 18 miles outside Olgii; however, this is mere speculation. No one really knows why the monoliths were used. Perhaps they are some type of marker.

Less than 50 yards away is a burial mound covered with rocks that appear to have been placed carefully on the site. The site itself is about four feet high and has a diameter of perhaps ten feet. These burial mounds are called "hirgisuur" – which means Kirjiz corpse. The Kirjiz were Turkic people who lived in what is now Mongolia.

As we climb back into our jeep and head back toward Olgii – suddenly Ganaa, my translator spots a fox on the hillside. Shinai, a local journalist, shakes Ganaa's hand and tells her today is our lucky day. According to Mongolian legend – if someone spots a fox or a wolf and it is moving adjacent to that person – it'll bring that person good luck.

By the time we stop, the fox has rounded the top of the hill and is out of sight. The driver refuses to give up. He starts the jeep and drives around the foot of the hill to the other side – where we see the fox again – climbing higher onto the hillside and then across the top. He is long gone, but just ahead we spot another stone monolith. This one is shorter, but nearby are more burial grounds.

We continue driving for another 15 minutes and come upon a ger sitting near the dry riverbed. We stop and get out. Shinai recognizes the owner and he invites us in for lunch. But since we don't have a lot of time we have snacks instead: ice cold homemade yogurt, curds and flour dough cookies. I dip the cookies into the yogurt – it's quite tasty. I pass on the curds – they are rock hard. The ger is decorated with traditional Kazakh wall hangings above two of the three beds – and around the bottom of the beds are hand-sewn cloth hangings. The owner's wife made all of the hangings.

After a short visit, we are back in the jeep and after passing a small herd of camels we come to a wide river that winds through the valley – where a major battle had taken place during the Mongolian war for independence in 1921. On a nearby hill, a white monument stands to honor the war hero General Hasbaatar – who fell in battle on that spot.

The driver pulls the jeep to the riverside and Shinai pulls a bottle of vodka from a plastic bag – along with some horsemeat, pickles, bread and water. We have a picnic in the jeep – with Shinai cutting the meat with his homemade knife. The meat tastes like roast beef – very tender and very flavorful. I welcome the vodka since it helps to warm me up. We sit by the river watching chunks of ice move swiftly downstream as the sun turns the upper two thirds of the distant mountain a bright red.

The driver and another journalist, Ospan, grab their fishing equipment and head for the river – braving the cold weather. The vodka no doubt helps. But after about 20 minutes they return empty-handed. The fish aren't biting. Ospan says there's too much ice in the river. We have another round of vodka, the driver starts the jeep and we are back on the road into town.

We get dropped off outside the black market. The temperature has dropped a few more degrees below zero, but the locals don't seem to notice. Dozens of people sit in their stalls selling everything from toothpaste to turnips. We are on a mission to buy horsemeat for Ganaa's friends back in Ulaanbaatar.

Ospan is with us and assures us he knows the best place to buy it.

We meet one of the food inspectors outside the meat market. Ospan says this man is a connoisseur of horsemeat and he gladly leads us into the building – where the smell of raw meat is almost breathtaking. Meat sellers stand behind their counters displaying whole sheep, horse hindquarters and beef. Down at the far end of the counter Ganaa sees what she is looking for: kaz – salted horsemeat stuffed inside horse intestines – and shaped into the form of a circular horse collar. Nearly a dozen "collars" are hanging on hooks dangling from the ceiling.

Our connoisseur touches each kaz – evaluating the quality. He spends about ten minutes doing so – until he settles on one. The seller cuts the string and the kaz drops into a plastic bag. The price: three US dollars – and enough horsemeat to feed about eleven people.

Now, we have to get the horsemeat on the plane back to UB. Ganaa doesn't want to carry it on and we have enough to carry already – including three dombra – a two-stringed traditional Kazak musical instrument and our backpacks.

Suddenly, I have a thought: Bayar had left a piece of his luggage with us and we both eyed it and grinned. He would never know, but he'd kill us if he ever found out. We begin to wrap the horsemeat collar in four plastic bags – and grab Bayar's sleeping bag and wrap the meat inside his bag and then stuff it into the sleeping bag's draw bag. It bulges a little bit more than normal, but otherwise it's a perfect fit.

At the airport, the MIAT security guard doesn't even look twice as the bag moves through the X-ray machine before being loaded onto the flight back to UB.

The sleeping bag served as an ideal storage container and not a bit of the horsemeat spilled into the bag. There was a slight lingering smell of meat in the bag after we removed it, but as far as I know, Bayar never learned the truth.

October 10, 2003

A Night at the Opera

The State Opera House is one of the first buildings that caught my eye when I arrived in Ulaanbaatar nearly four months ago. It was built in the early 1960's during the Soviet period, a huge pastel orange building with giant white columns in the front and wide balconies on the sides. It sits very prominently on the southeast corner of the city's main gathering spot – Sukhbaatar Square.

The square, itself, is a miniaturized version of Beijing's Tiananmen Square or Moscow's Red Square. Until renovations, it had been a huge, somewhat neglected paved space. Its centerpiece is a giant statue of revolutionary hero Sukhbaatar on horseback facing east. At the time, a bright green six foot high fence had been placed around the square – while construction crews resurfaced the area and replaced the asphalt with a smooth brick.

Before the green fence went up, I used to sit on benches near the foot of the statue. People would come up and sit next to me. Some wanted to practice English. Others want to sell me things – everything from knock-off Rolex watches to "genuine" dinosaur eggs.

It was the opera house that always caught my eye when I sat in the square.

One day I got a chance to go inside.

A huge chandelier hangs in the auditorium around it, painted on the ceiling are pastel greens, pinks, reds and purples, forming what, at first glance, appears to be a lotus petal, but it is instead the Mongolian national symbol.

The hall, while imposing on the outside, is actually small and intimate inside. Those sitting on the front row can literally reach out and touch the conductor. Parents sit with small children in their laps and the youngsters applaud enthusiastically at the appropriate moments. Some of the children have fiery red cheeks; the wind-burn is an indication they spend a lot of time outdoors.

Sitting in the second row is a man in a suit and tie; behind him is an elderly man wearing a traditional del – a long sheepskin lined coat worn by herders as well as some urbanites. This man is leaning forward totally entranced by the action on stage.

Who would have thought that a nomadic, animal herding people, who live in small round tents on a vast open plain, would be interested in the romantic excesses of Verdi's La Traviata?

It's my second visit to the State Opera house.

The previous night I had attended a ballet and my seat was near the back of the hall in a special box-seat area that I shared with a Chinese prima ballerina and her male partner, who sat to my right. They will be the main performers in the Swan Lake ballet later in the week. The young man told me it was his first time in Mongolia even though his father is Mongolian. He and his partner are from Guangzhou, China.

I asked him what he thought about while he was on stage and he told me he is always nervous at first, concentrating on his moves. Later, he conceded that he sometimes daydreams while on stage.

Behind me were four young Japanese girls – who'll perform in the opera and ballet festival later in the week -- and to my left were two middle-aged Russian men – the one closest to me is a conductor. They talked quietly during much of the performance and at one point – I heard the man nearest me mouthing the words of one of the male opera singers on stage. (Three nights later I watched him conduct the ballet Giselle) He is also apparently a heavy smoker as stale smoke seemed to ooze from his light blue suit.

Throughout the evening – out in the audience, mobile phones are chiming, playing songs and making funny tones. It's almost as if there are two operas going on at the same time: La Traviata on stage and La Telephone in the audience.

At one point, a tiny bright light catches my eye just below me. It's the blue screen of a mobile phone. A young woman is typing out a text message to someone – is it her own lover perhaps? On stage, Alfredo Germont is confessing his love to Violetta Valery.

Through the music and ring tones we eventually arrive at the death scene – where Germont, played by a Chinese singer, is making final plans with his lover, Violetta, who is played by a Russian diva. Violetta is dying of tuberculosis and suddenly she falls dead at Germont's feet. It is an emotional scene because the couple has just reconciled after a bitter misunderstanding. Their voices are superb together, but the singer who may have stolen the show is Dr. Grenvil's character. Khavlaagh is from Mongolia's Kazak region and his baritone voice is rich and mesmerizing.

I never dreamed I would watch a romantic Italian opera in an authoritarian-style opera house at the edge of the Earth. That thought makes me smile as I walk into the theater, but as the performance begins, I am soon transported to Violetta's salon in Paris.

Mongolians take their opera seriously. The performance was first-class.

The North Korean Circus

She is dangling upside down on a swing 40 feet above me – her heels are somehow carefully balanced on the cross bar, all that is keeping her from plunging to the ground. As if the balancing act weren't enough to amaze those watching, she suddenly starts juggling three tennis balls – all the while – clinched between her teeth is a ten foot long metal pole with a small chandelier pointing skyward.

It is the "World Famous Dream Circus" direct from Pyongyang, North Korea. I had been invited to the circus and was told it was a Korean circus. I had assumed it was from South Korea. North Korea's Dream Circus first performed in Ulaanbaatar 30 years ago – and UB has been a stop on its world tour ever since.

This circus is all acrobats.

A woman reclines in a chair with her feet straight up in the air – flipping and turning two three-foot long sparkling cylinders. She uses her feet like hands – and she exudes total confidence. She is totally in control as her assistant exchanges the cylinders for five volleyballs – which she immediately begins to juggle with her hands and feet – eventually tossing each one into a huge basket. She concludes with an amazing stunt. Her prop is a 15-foot long pole with five flat steps sticking out; at the top is a small basket. Using one foot to balance the pole, she uses her other foot to toss a volleyball onto the first step. Next, using her foot to move the pole up and down, she bounces the ball all the way up the steps and eventually into the basket.

The grand finale features a team of eight acrobats doing double and triple flips 50 feet above the audience. Timing, of course, is everything when swinging from one platform to another. In a nearly 30 minute performance, only one acrobat missed the mark, plunging into the net below as the audience let out a collective gasp. He quickly climbs back up and does a perfect triple flip to a standing ovation.

A huge North Korean flag hangs from the side of the circus wall – at times the shadows of the acrobats appear on the flag as they swing back and forth from the rafters.

At one point during the evening – assistants bring out several tall metal cylinders and place them on a platform near the center of the ring. I assume it is for the next act, but oddly – no sooner have the cylinders been brought out – they mysteriously disappear.

Preparing to leave, I dig my USA 2002 Olympics beret from my jacket pocket and place it on my head as the acrobats parade around the ring after the performance. One of the male acrobats looks in my direction and I mouth the word "bravo" and smile. He returns the smile and bows slightly before waving goodbye to the audience and disappearing behind the curtain.

October 18, 2003

Inside a Mongolian Prison

I went to prison today.

As I step through the dark narrow passage, a guard stands to my left and holds the heavy iron gate open for me. Inside, is warmth and sunlight and a huge yard – with three brightly colored miniature wooden benches and tables with umbrellas. Nearby is a big metal tank resting on four poles with a water spigot dangling over a series of small wooden compartments that serves as outdoor showers in the summer months. The yard is peaceful – except for the occasional squawking crow.

Zaisan Juvenile Prison number 411 sits halfway up a beautiful valley that overlooks Ulaanbaatar. It is home to about 120 boys between the ages of 14 and 18. Ten percent of them are homeless. Their crimes include murder, sexual assault, robbery and shoplifting. Prison director Tsanjid tells me the vast majority of the boys have been convicted of robbery. And that about five percent will wind up back in Zaisan or in an adult prison after they turn 18.

Seventeen-year-old Mungun Hyag has done two years of a three-year sentence for robbery. He is personable as I speak to him through a translator. He had been working quietly in the yard and our guide, Dulmaa, had called him over to chat with us. Mungun tells me his parents and siblings do not visit him, but adds he will be moving home when he gets out next year. He says he was living on the streets of UB when he was arrested.

Mungun says he was beaten and kicked in the neck and shoulders by the police after he was handcuffed. He tells me he wasn't seriously injured, but was bruised by the beating. There is no way to know whether

Mungun is being truthful, but he said this in response to a question I asked after our guide had disappeared into a building.

As we were leaving, Mungun asks if he can ask us a question. He put one hand over his mouth and whispered "will you give me some money."

"Why," I ask.

"Because I need to buy shoes," he exclaims.

"Doesn't the prison provide you with shoes?" I ask.

"No, the inmates' parents or relatives must bring shoes and clothing," he says in a matter of fact tone as he looks down at his plastic sandals with thick gray socks.

"What size shoe do you wear," I then ask.

"Size 40," he replies.

He then asks for two-thousand tugrug – a little less than two US dollars, but I don't give him any money.

I ask him what inmates often do with the money their relatives give them. "We buy cigarettes," he replies.

We make our way toward a long two-story building on the south end of the yard with tall pine trees planted across the front. As we enter the lobby, straight ahead and through a glass wall, I can see eight to ten bunks in a large room. The inmates are busy sweeping, mopping and dusting.

As we climb the steps to the second floor, the smell of fresh paint fills my lungs. Even the steps had been painted: a bright yellow with an even brighter green trim along the edges. The bright yellow color scheme continues as we walk into a long hallway – where a teenager is using a razor blade to scrap paint off a windowpane. I ask our guide, Dulmaa, who is a teacher at the prison, why the inmate is allowed to have such a potentially deadly instrument. "They are given out to specific prisoners and are returned at the end of the day," she replies as she pointed toward a doorway.

Inside, several inmates are hanging large pieces of artwork. It is mainly traditional landscapes – painted in pastels and consisting of wide-open spaces with an occasional ger off to the right or left.

Dulmaa leads us down the long hallway and informs us that this area is devoted to vocational training – gardening, handicrafts and carpet making. She says the students work from 9 a.m. until 1 p.m. each day, but today, each of the rooms is empty and locked.

At the other end of the hall is a small library. It too is empty. The desks and chairs are neatly arranged with bookshelves on each side of the wall.

The children's prison opened in 1995 in a converted hospital. The west end of the building now serves as the prison hospital. There are two nurses on duty today and three or four inmates are pushing mops, brooms and paint brushes. On the walls are dozens of health messages, including one urging its readers to practice safe sex to avoid getting HIV AIDS.

While we only get to see a glimpse of where the inmates are housed, I am surprised to find the prison so bright – not just from the paint job; huge windows allow in plenty of sunlight. Prison director Tsanjid tells me "we are painting the prison in bright colors and allowing in lots of sunshine so that the hearts of the prisoners will become bright and sunny."

I leave with a positive impression of the juvenile prison, but I have to admit, I wonder if we are only seeing the "nice" parts. I also am a bit skeptical about the vocational training courses. The training room appeared untouched. It felt more like a stage prop than something that gets used on a regular basis.

Khenti

The shallow snow in the ruts of the road glistens like silk in the morning sun as we make our way from Khenti back to Ulaanbaatar. The driver, Batsaihkhan, has chosen a short cut that hasn't been used since the last snowfall several days earlier. The pure white snow covers the dirt path that parallels the electric lines stretching as far as the eye can see across the eastern Mongolian steppe.

This road, like most in Mongolia, is strewn with rusty scrap metal, tires and a little bit of everything else. There's an entire axle rod off to the left, straight ahead and just off the road to the right is a vodka bottle that has been emptied and left standing upright, further along someone has stuck a steel rod in the ground and placed a steering wheel on top. It gives the appearance of a spinning top frozen in time. Bits of coal and pieces of sheep hide lay scattered about – having fallen off the old Russian trucks that traverse these paths daily – bringing supplies from UB out to the eastern towns and villages.

As we drive due west, weaving our way through the electric poles, I spot about two dozen tiny tombstones some 100 yards off the roadway. They appear to be about 12 inches high. There is no fence to keep out the livestock that are grazing nearby. It is a peaceful place, but it also makes me feel lonely. The graveyard is very isolated and I wonder if relatives ever visit their family members there on that grassy hillside. There are no gers anywhere in sight. It is another 30 kilometers before we see the next village.

Cruising into this village, I am reminded of a Hollywood set. There are storefronts in the long line of single story buildings – mainly dwellings that offer home cooked meals. A couple of horses are tied up outside next to an old Russian logging truck. We pull up to a building that has a huge satellite dish out front and a new Sharp television sitting inside on one of the tables.

Two young women are cooking by a crackling fire in the side room the only means of heat for the restaurant. A toddler with a bad hair day and a runny nose is waddling from table to table. She smiles when we offer her some cookies. She shares them with her mom – who is boiling us some milk tea.

It is bitter cold outside – about 20 below zero Celsius – and the single pane of glass is iced over at the top and bottom. The room, however, is surprisingly warm – even without any heat.

Outside the window, a dozen or so dogs wander about – scattering as more truck drivers pull their dusty rigs up to the front of the building. They get out and check the tires, the axles and peer under the hood before shuffling into the restaurant – kicking the mud and dirt off their boots just before stepping inside.

I am struck by how Mongolians seemingly get used to this bitter cold. When I step outside I am bundled up in six or seven layers of clothing, but Mongolians appear to be wearing only two or three. It is no doubt their diet helps keep them warm. They are downing lots of hot milk tea and platefuls of fat.

As we are leaving the restaurant, two truckers ask the cook to make them some Tsuivan – fried homemade noodles with vegetables and mutton. They shout – "have you got some fat you can put in it?" And she replies, "sure and we've got sheep tail, too!" The truckers smile and immediately order two extra large portions.

Author's Note: The road from Ulaanbaatar to Khenti is now a two-lane paved road.

The Snow Men of Darkhan

Twenty men wearing orange reflector vests are busy digging in the middle of the icy road with shovels, long steel bars and hoes. They are Mongolia's answer to the snowplow. As one chops the ice into small chunks – another man grabs a shovel full and tosses it to the side of the road. Still another uses a broom to sweep away the remaining debris.

It is late morning and the temperature is around 20 below zero Celsius as our Land Cruiser makes its way from Ulaanbaatar north some 200 kilometers to Darkhan, Mongolia's second largest city. The road is intermittently clean of ice and snow where these work crews have chipped their way down to the asphalt.

The size of these work crews range from as many as a dozen men to as few as one man working a seemingly endless stretch of ice-covered highway – with just a steel rod and shovel. I was told that a 12-person crew can clear about one and a half kilometers of roadway in an eight hour day. I find that amazing and somehow doubt that is possible.

I admire their determination in this seemingly impossible and never-ending job. They are paid to clear away the ice and snow, but the pay isn't much. It's about the equivalent of two and one half dollars per day.

These crews are a familiar sight all over Mongolia – year round. In late spring, summer and early autumn, they're busy with long brooms – literally sweeping the dirt and dust into the gutter and then down into storm drains.

Both men and women work as street sweepers. I even saw one woman in her orange reflector vest and dress pants wearing high heels. Maybe it was her part time job before she goes off to the office.

Some street sweepers work down the center lane of traffic – ignoring the chaotic car horns around them. They appear to be in their own world as they work their brooms as if they're extensions of their bodies – using a lull in traffic to sweep the debris from the center to the side of the road.

Here in Darkhan, children as young as 15 are deployed to clean the streets and sidewalks. They, too, work their tools like professionals – lifting and dropping a long steel rod to break up the ice – while another student uses a shovel to remove the broken parts. A third follows with a broom to sweep any remaining ice off the roadway.

The long steel rods leave tiny pockmarks in the road. As we bump over a stretch of newly cleaned roadway, the taxi driver points at the street and says "look at this. It's a new road and it's been destroyed by the road crews and their tools."

It is back-breaking work and it doesn't take long for exhaustion to set in. Work crews begin chopping and clearing away the ice around 7 or 8 a.m. By midmorning, they have cleared perhaps 20 yards of street.

One man clearly had had enough for a while. I spot him lying on his side on the ice, smiling at his workmates as he takes a long, slow drag on his cigarette. The cold air and ice don't seem to penetrate his body or his mind.

November 11, 2003

Stuffing Ourselves around Baya Nuur

I will remember November 21, 2002 as the day of the five feasts.

It begins with a 120-kilometer ride from the town of Olgii to the village of Bayan Nuur – nestled among giant red boulders and alongside the meandering and icy Hovd River in western Mongolia. With a population of less than 600 people, the village provides more than 50 percent of Bayan Olgii's fruits and vegetables.

World Vision's Terry Cornelison and I are traveling with the Aimag's (province) agriculture minister and our first stop is the village governor's office for introductions. Terry is investigating the possibility of working with the local community on horticulture and animal husbandry projects. This makes Terry the big celebrity in town and all the government types are going to make sure we have everything we need.

After the short meeting, we drive to the governor's house for a lunch of mutton, curds, cabbage slaw, milk tea, cookies and chocolates. The coleslaw is my favorite dish and I go back for seconds as Ganaa, my translator, and Terry keep reaching for the mutton – the centerpiece of the meal on a big metal tray. Terry has lived in Mongolia for a number of years and is used to eating fatty mutton. The lunch concludes with the host bringing out a bottle of vodka – proudly made in Bayan Olgii – for a series of toasts.

With the vodka warming us up, we step outside into the minus-15-degree weather for a tour of a small fruit tree farm. The four feet tall trees have been wrapped in clothing to keep them from freezing. From a distance, they look like children playing. Afterward, much to our surprise, we are invited into the owner's home where another huge meal is laid out for us. It is similar to the first, but this time we eat less. At the end, however, there is more vodka and more toasts.

Next stop: another vegetable grower who has a root cellar filled with heads of cabbage and potatoes. Terry purchases five kilos of potatoes for about one US dollar. As he loads the potatoes into our truck, the family is inviting us in for yet another meal.

This spread is the biggest yet – with similar dishes, but also two huge jars of tomato preserve. It's delicious and I spread it on the homemade bread that the owner's wife brings out. She tells me the preserve is easy to make: "just boil some tomatoes and add some sugar and then boil them together."

Her brother in law, a burly man with a big smile and a head of short white hair, tells us stories about driving between Olgii and Almaty, Kazakhstan. He says he makes the run in about 20 days – driving a Russian minivan. On the way, he has to drive 1200 kilometers through Russia – and says he has to pay bribes all along the way – ranging anywhere from two to three US dollars. Despite the bribes, he says he still makes a profit of about 500 US dollars per trip.

What we believe is our fourth and final lunch is at the Agriculture Minister's home. It's a traditional Kazakh meal, and for Terry and me, the honored guests, he has prepared the sheep's head. We were each given a piece of the sheep's cheek. Next, he removed one of the ears and hands it to Ganaa.

As I take a big sigh of relief, Ganaa's eyes grow wide and she isn't sure what to do. As she stares at the blackened ear in her hands, the Ag Minister tells her that since she's the youngest person at the table, it is tradition that she should eat it.

She looks at me for help, but I have to admit I'm only glad it isn't me who is left holding the ear. After holding it in her hands for a few seconds – and while no one is looking, Ganaa quickly and quietly slips the ear back on the meat platter – in front of the sheep's head. Fortunately for all of us, there would be no vodka served at meal number four.

The Ag Minister is a strict Muslim.

The ministry official suggests we take a ride into the countryside before our fifth and final meal. He says it'll help settle our previous four meals and wet our appetites for the next one.

We travel more than a dozen kilometers south of Bayan Nuur to a huge plain next to the Hovd River. Standing in the middle of the plain is what the locals called Stone Man – a seven-foot high stone carving that may have been erected in the 6th or 7th century. His eyes are a bit faded, but his smile is intact and so is his intricately carved stone belt. It is believed that an important official is buried nearby – and that Stone Man was erected to serve as a marker for the grave.

The village governor suggests that maybe Genghis Khan himself is buried there. No one actually knows his actual burial place, but it's enough of an excuse for the village chief to bring out a bottle of Genghis vodka. He tells us it's a tradition to drink with Stone Man – so the bottle was put to Stone Man's lips and he symbolically has a sip.

The bottle is then passed around the living for a few toasts.

As we drive back toward town, the sun is quickly dropping behind the ridges – giving the snow-capped mountains to the east – a purplish glow. It also means the temperature is dropping as fast as the sun – and the wind is picking up.

Just south of town, we stop again.

We tour a four-acre farm of cabbages and fruit trees and then are invited into a hand-made brick house for the final feast. There is no electricity in or around the village. So, the entire house is dark – except for the glow being emitted from the kitchen stove and two candles on the dining table covered with food.

As our group of eight or nine sit around the table – the candlelight dances on everyone's face. On the table, are home-made pickles, tomato preserves, a turnip and garlic salad and bottomless bowls of milk tea. As we begin to eat, the Ag Minister keeps glancing at his watch. Not quite sundown – not officially anyway.

The farmer's wife walks into the room with a huge wooden bowl. It is a family heirloom and it's covered by a bed of shredded cabbage and onions – with some type of meat on top.

It's chicken and her timing is impeccable – the Ag Minister looks at his watch once again – smiles, steps away to wash his hands, returns and reaches for a fork. Being a strict Muslim, he's observing Ramadan and has been fasting since sun-up. Confirming by his watch that the sun has set, he can join the feast.

After dinner, a young man enters the room carrying a guitar – he sings a traditional Kazakh song and follows it up with a Mongolian one. Then, the group looks at Terry and me and Ganaa translates: "it is customary for the guests to sing now." After a few seconds, Terry suggests "Swing Low, Sweet Chariot" and we give it our all. Our audience is too kind – afterward, they suggest we take our song on the road -- down to the local club for a try out. We graciously decline.

We drive back to Olgii that evening stuffed with mutton, beef, chicken, vegetables and fruit. Along the way, we stop to stretch our legs and as we walk about the silence of the night sounds beautiful. It's an incredibly clear night. Terry spots a shooting star, Ganaa points to a satellite moving quickly across the star-filled sky, Mars is bright and moving higher and the Big Dipper sits low on the horizon just above the jagged mountain peaks that surround us.

I feel like I won't need to eat again for at least a week.

November 16, 2003

Sub-Zero Soccer

The temperature is hovering around minus 10 and I am watching a soccer game in an outdoor stadium in Ulaanbaatar where the snow is piled four feet high along the sidelines. And it actually doesn't feel that cold!

It must be the energy in the stands that makes it feel warmer than it is. Several hundred Mongolians have turned out to cheer the home team to victory against Maldives – a series of tropical islands that stretch from the southwestern tip of India all the way to equator. Those guys must be freezing their shorts off, but I can't tell just by watching them play.

I assume the Mongolians have the advantage being used to the cold – and the team from Maldives initially must feel the same way. Someone comments that Team Maldives almost conceded the game, but at the last minute decided to experience soccer in sub-zero weather.

Both teams are dressed in regular uniforms – shorts and short sleeve shirts. However, they also are wearing gloves and camel hair leggings on their arms and legs. Some of the Maldivian players also wear red knit caps with their green uniforms.

Admittedly, the whole thing is too surreal. That's why I decided to head to the stadium to watch at least some of the game.

I'm not disappointed.

Just 24 hours earlier the field had been covered with several inches of snow. Overnight and early that morning, a team of sweepers had worked magic – and found the green grass. Yet, as the players run along the field, they leave small dust storms of snow behind them. But neither side appears to notice the cold. In fact, most of the players are sweating. The players on the sidelines wait inside warm minivans. In the stands – there's a constant roar.

Over the last few weeks, I've come to realize just how tough and rugged Mongolians are. The cold doesn't seem to bother most people. It's more a minor inconvenience.

Lots of cars refuse to start when it's below zero; some drivers cover the hoods and fronts of their trucks and cars with animal skins. The asphalt does strange things in sub-zero weather; it puckers into tiny cones that drivers try to avoid for fear of puncturing a tire.

It's not unusual to see breakdowns in the middle of the street. And it's normal to see the drivers – with only their legs sticking out from under the vehicle – using their bare hands and a wrench to try to get their vehicle moving again in the sub-zero cold.

As they work under their cars – other men and women pound away at the ice on the streets and sidewalks – using crowbars and shovels to clear it away. No sooner have they cleared a path than it snows again and they start all over refusing to surrender to the severe will of Mother Nature.

Much to my regret, I have yet to learn to do the Mongolian shuffle. It is something of a dance that people do as they walk to keep from slipping on the ice. I have resumed my dance lessons after falling hard on my hip and elbow. Nothing broken, but I have a renewed sense of respect for the ice. I take it very slowly – almost on all fours.

Mongolians, however, have an amazing sense of balance. I rarely see anyone fall – even women wearing high-heels seem to move quite quickly along the sidewalks. It is a fascinating ice dance that I watch each morning and afternoon on my way to and from work, but first I have to scrape away the ice buildup on the inside of the taxi windows. And I also have to wait until the condensation evaporates on my contact lenses. It's just like what happens to your glasses when you step from the cold into a heated space.

My lungs sting from the subzero weather and I often cough the instant I step back into the cold. The ice and snow make a loud crunching sound as I walk; cars and trucks make strange groaning noises. I often see people with ice frozen on the tips of their eyelashes and eyebrows. Yet, many people seem immune to the cold – or they just ignore it -- laughing and carrying on casual conversations with their friends as they scoot or shuffle their feet over the icy sidewalks.

So, yes, I am fascinated by the cold and the way Mongolians cope and that's probably why I am sitting, sometimes standing, on the edge of this soccer field watching a game played in subzero weather.

It's a bad day for the Mongolians – even with the home field and sub-zero advantage. The Maldivians score the only point in the game. Still, the Mongolians do have something to look forward to. Tomorrow Team Mongolia will board a plane for Maldives to thaw out and trade their camel hair leggings for suntan lotion.

December 6, 2003

Holiday in Mongolia

For weeks, the neighbor who lives on the other side of my bedroom wall has been practicing Rachmaninov on their piano. Suddenly, this morning, it becomes Jingle Bells.

It's yet another sign that it's beginning to sound as well as look a lot like Christmas in Mongolia – never mind that most Mongolians are Tibetan Buddhists.

Over the past two weeks or so, I've noticed a huge blow up Santa go up outside a shop on my street. (He has since been deflated). A life-size Santa with wire-rimmed glasses has been given a prominent place in my bank's lobby. He shakes his hips and says "ho, ho, ho!" And a camera shop has a 12-foot high snowman made of large chunks of ice and snow on the sidewalk out front of their store. He probably won't melt until next May.

I am enjoying these familiar holiday symbols and the new snowfall, too. The snow especially makes it seem even more like home.

I am one of a handful of expats who is spending the holidays in Mongolia. Most have left for home. For me, it's exciting and sometimes surprising to experience Mongolia at holiday time. Taxis have attached thick pieces of tinsel to their car antennas, others had five-inch Santa's on their dashboards. The State Department Store, the biggest shopping center and a hold-over from Soviet times, has set aside a whole section of the store to sell artificial trees and all the holiday trimmings.

Mistletoe, sometimes the real stuff, dangles from restaurant ceilings. Occasionally, the radio stations play Christmas music. And portraits of the jolly, old man in red have sprung up all over the city.

Santa Claus is called Winter Man in Mongolia. He wears a blue del (a del is traditional Mongolian clothing and is like a long robe) and a white cloak with a blue hat with white fur trimming. I haven't yet spotted Winter Man, and I'm told he won't make an appearance until around New Year's Day. I'll be looking for him – because just like old Saint Nick, Winter Man gives out presents.

There are lots of parties and performances.

Many offices, for instance, put on skits. On Christmas night, the staff at my office, The Gobi Initiative, puts on an extremely funny soap opera – complete with costumes and music. (I know it's funny, I have watched the rehearsals!) The previous year – there was a variety show of sorts – featuring contortionists, a rendition of Swan Lake and traditional Mongolian dance, but I'm told the best performance prize went to the Gobi Initiative drivers. They dressed in tights and tutus and performed "The Flight of the Bumble Bee."

One of my favorite events, so far, is ice sculpting. Mongolians take it very seriously. I'm talking about gigantic sculptures.

There's a young princess sitting on a camel that is two stories high and 40 feet long. There are delicately sculpted dragons standing 15 feet high with large fangs, larger than life lions and an exquisite Garuda - - the mythical bird from the Indian epic, The Mahabharata.

The buzz of chainsaws, axes striking ice and workers shouting instructions to each other can be heard over the roar of Russian-made tanker trucks. These trucks are loaded with water – which is then pumped into barrels where workers carry the water in pails to their ice creations.

Keep in mind, this work is going on outside – where the temperature is hovering just below zero Celsius.

The workers hardly notice the frigid temperatures, dozens of them are too busy getting a dragon's fang just right or making sure the princess' crown is straight. The temperature is actually ideal for ice-sculpting.

It is late afternoon and the last few minutes of sunlight have turned the ice boulders that have yet to be sculpted into large glistening diamonds. Nearby, one worker – wearing a thick coat and large mittens – is taking a smoke break – a cigarette in one hand and his ice sculpting axe in the other. He is staring at his creation – no doubt thinking about his next stroke.

Mongolia has inspired me as an artist. I started a series of Mongolian paintings last summer – using birch trees as a theme. I have continued to use the birches in all nine of my pieces. I have watched my palette change from lots of greens to grays, whites and blue.

For me, the Mongolian sky in winter is almost indescribable. It is a spectacular deep blue. It reminds me of the New Mexico sky that Georgia O'Keefe used to paint. A sky that I had thought was only in O'Keefe's imagination until I visited New Mexico.

Like in New Mexico, the Mongolian sky looks surreal – and at the same time it feels comforting. Perhaps I associate such a deep blue sky with warmth and for that reason – the ultramarine sky makes the frigid weather seem less so.

December 22, 2003

94

Mongolian Cuisine, Navigating the Ice and Taxis

Everyone warned me about the food in Mongolia when they learned I would be moving here for nine months. It was always the same remark "I hope you like boiled mutton." One friend even gave me a bottle of Tabasco sauce and wrote on it: "Mutton Enhancement Sauce." It is true that Mongolia is not a likely place to find a gastronomic delight, but it is possible. It just takes a little detective work.

Taj Mahal does offer consistently decent Indian food. I especially enjoy the thal at lunchtime. The tandoor chicken with herbs and spices is tasty, too – as are the breads. Some Indian restaurants make their breads too oily. That is not the case at Taj Mahal. The plain naan – which I always order -- is baked with tender loving care.

The restaurant had been hidden away in an alley behind the enormous Soviet-era sports palace, but moved into a hotel and was a bit easier to find. Now, it has moved again as the hotel undergoes renovations. During my time in Mongolia, some of the better restaurants in Ulaanbaatar were like hidden gems waiting to be discovered.

Millie's, an expat hangout, with excellent burgers, tacos and lasagna is 100 yards off the main road – located behind one of a handful of monasteries that survived the purges of the 1930's. It's a pleasant, but slippery walk in winter. The alley parallels the western wall of the monastery – which is now called the Choijin Lama Museum.

By far the best Korean barbeque in town is at Seoul Restaurant. It too is off the beaten path – located on the edge of Children's Park. The park had been a neglected patch of land that must have been beautiful at one time. Inside the park were faded statues of each of the 12 lunar calendar animals – behind them was a beautiful mosaic depicting several

Mongolian folk tales – further east were several rusted amusement rides that still worked.

The Ferris wheel was a great place to watch the sun set in summer and early fall -- and the ride turned extremely slowly. Once around cost the equivalent of 50 cents.

A few years after my departure, the amusement rides, including the Ferris wheel, were removed and now a private company operates the children's park.

No, it is not good food that I miss in Mongolia, but there are a couple of other things that I have come to yearn for and surprisingly so. They are rain and the melting of ice and snow.

It is too cold for either.

The sidewalks have been coated in a solid sheet of ice for about two months now. It is more than an inch thick in many places. And where it has been cleared away – the occasional marble sidewalks are still treacherous. I fear the slippery marble more than the ice. And the new fallen snow makes a walk even more dangerous. The snow covers up the marble and leaves you wondering (until you slip) whether you are walking on concrete or marble.

Crossing the street in UB is risky any time of year because pedestrians have no rights, but in winter it's even more dangerous. You can't run across the streets because of the ice – and the cars and trucks can barely stop for the same reason – and most vehicles are riding on bald tires -- making it virtually impossible to stop quickly.

Hailing a cab in winter requires patience and warm clothing. Rush hour regularly means a 15-minute wait and when the cab actually stops – it's a good idea to step back – the car often slides 20 or 30 feet down the icy street before stopping. Once inside, the heater may not work, so if it's a long ride it's best to dress in layers. And going up a hill in a taxi can be a very slow process, but somehow the drivers almost always make it to the top – zigging and zagging their way around an obstacle course of other spinning vehicles.

I admire these cabbies.

They work in extreme conditions – coping with icy streets, sometimes no heat and more times than not -- passengers who've had a little too much vodka. It's not surprising that most cabbies have a blue silk scarf draped above their sun visors. It's a Buddhist tradition; they strongly believe it helps them to have a safe journey. So far, my journeys in the taxis of UB have been relatively safe – and definitely entertaining, particularly when I am searching for those hidden gems of restaurants in the back alleys and out of the way spots of Ulaanbaatar.

December 31, 2003

New Year's Day in Khangai, Mongolia

As the sun comes up on New Year's Day 2004, I am standing by a huge bonfire on the Mongolian steppe as the temperature hovers around 35 below zero. It's exhilarating and unlike any New Year I have ever experienced.

For one thing, I am not normally awake at sunrise on New Year's morning. My adventure began at 4:30 a.m. when my alarm went off. Somehow, I find my way out of bed and make it to the train station. Then, I climb aboard a special train at Ulaanbaatar that takes me and about 30 others to greet the sun some 40 kilometers southeast of the capital.

On this trip, I am joined by half a dozen friends. Each of us has our own compartment, food and bottle of bubbly. Nevertheless, we squeeze into one compartment where we commence to drink Mimosas, eat smoked salmon, caviar, hard boiled eggs, fresh bread and chocolates – as the train slowly makes its way through the darkness.

Two hours later, we begin to see the outline of several ridges off in the distance – everything in between is covered with a blanket of snow.

It's cozy in our warm compartment -- thanks in large part to Mary Fran, who has handled logistics for our trip. She has thought of everything – even on two hours sleep -- a knife for the cheese and salami, pliers – just in case the champagne cork gets stuck, glasses, a small cooler and orange juice for the mimosas.

As I was munching on smoked salmon, cheese and bread, my friend, Jim, suddenly shouts, "check it out." We all make for the window and spot a raging bonfire – 20 yards from the train. We have arrived.

As I climb down from the train, the icy air hits my face and stings my lungs. After a brief coughing fit, I take a deep breath. The cold air feels fresh and clean in my lungs. It's a refreshing break from the smog in UB – caused, in large measure, by all the ger camps huddled around the city – where residents burn brown coal for heat.

The eastern sky is already streaked with shades of pink as the sun is just moments from climbing above the horizon. Behind me, the snow-covered hills are turning shades of purple. It's a spectacular moment – and I step away from the others to listen to the silence of the new morning.

I watch in silence as the hills around me keep changing colors while the sun continues its journey toward the horizon. Suddenly, as it pops into view – the sky around it turns a red orange – and then higher over the horizon a deep orange – and it slowly graduates to lighter shades of orange and soft pinks.

As I wonder back to the bonfire, the heat feels good on my cold fingers and face. Around me, several people are twirling sparklers – others are setting off fireworks. I wander back to the train, where a Mongolian band is warming up.

The mini-concert is held in the lounge car and features a morin khuur (horsehead fiddle), limbe (wooden flute) and a female singer. She sings long songs – a tradition in which the singer slowly pronounces the words and sometimes divides them into syllables. Afterward, a throat singer – someone who sings from deep within their throat and often creates two, sometimes three notes at the same time – takes the small stage – dressed in animal skins and a huge fur cap.

Throat singing is not easy to describe. One has to hear it. There are two main components. The first is a low, sustained pitch, similar to the drone of a bagpipe. The other, superimposed on the low drone, is a succession of flute-like sounds that resonate high above the drone. It is this component that can be controlled so as to mimic birds, the wind or insects.

It is astonishing to see and hear throat singing performed – and here I am on a train – on the Mongolian steppe – miles from any town -- listening to one of the finest performances I have ever experienced.

The sun is now higher in the deep blue sky and as I eat breakfast in the dining car – decorated with beautiful wood carvings – I pour each of my friends a glass of sparkling Russian wine. We clink our glasses and a huge grin appears on my face – as I thought about the incredible day and year so far. The others must be thinking the same thought. They grin, too, and we wish each other a Happy New Year.

Author's Note: *The special New Year's Day train excursion between Ulaanbaatar and Khangai no longer operates.*

January 1, 2004

Karakorum

As I sit near a crackling fire at the main temple at Karakorum, listening to the Buddhist monks chant their prayers in the Tibetan language, I am carried away to a place long ago and far away in my childhood.

The fire and the peacefulness of the chanting transport me back to Sunday afternoons at my Uncle Fred's house on Big Laurel in the mountains of western North Carolina. The chants are rhythmic -- reminding me of the ticking antique clock that sat on my uncle's mantle above the fireplace. The tick-tock of the clock would send me into something like a trance as he and my grandpa would quietly chat about old times and the week's news.

It's a comforting thought as I warm my hands over the stove in the 17th century temple that is home to only a fraction of the number of monks who used to pray here. Before the Stalinist purges of the 1930's, more than 1,000 Buddhist monks prayed at Erdene Zuu Monastery at Karakorum – the ancient capital of the Mongol Empire dating back to 1220.

As I walk around the massive compound surrounded by 108 white stupas, I try to imagine what it must have looked like before much of it was destroyed in the 1930's. Of the 62 original temples inside the compound – only ten remain. The three largest temples are each filled with beautiful artwork with giant golden Buddhas as the centerpiece. Two wooden columns in front of the Buddhas have hand carved dragons snaking their way up toward the ceiling. Along the walls are 15th century hand-painted scenes of heaven and hell, protecting angels and gods.

These three temples are not heated, but the icy air seems to melt away as I gaze in wonder at the artwork – some of which was painted with a single hair from a horse's tail. The minute detail is striking and inspiring.

Stepping back outside, there is a dark blue sky overhead – while snow covers much of the ground inside the compound. However, there are a few spots where beautiful rock art is visible – these stepping stones measure about one foot square. Within the squares small inlaid stones form sunrays – while a yellow stone in the center represents the sun, itself. They are so beautiful; I am reluctant to step on them. These 15th century sun-stones are representations of ancient Mongol coins.

Karakorum sits on a plain – and in the distance, beyond the stupas that form the wall around the compound, I can see bluish-gray tree-covered hills with patches of snow in the open spaces with the surreal sky as a backdrop.

I feel a deep sense of inner calm as the sunshine warms my face, the monks continue to chant in the distance and a faint smell of incense floats through the air. It is one of those special moments in time when I am totally in the moment – feeling very much alive and thankful.

The wind begins to pick up – stinging my face and reminding me that I am experiencing one of those "moments" in subzero weather. I smile at the thought – and begin to drift back. My fingers suddenly feel cold and I make my way through the gate and toward the warmth of the Jeep.

If you don't mind the cold, wintertime is a good time to visit Karakorum, located almost due west of Ulaanbaatar. On this particular day in late January I have the place to myself. As I slowly make my way around the compound – I try to imagine what life must have been like when this city was the center of the vast Mongol Empire that once stretched from Eastern Europe and parts of the Middle East to Manchuria and south to Indonesia.

January 30, 2004

The Town of Choibalsan and Mongolian Hotels

The vast flat space before me is almost overwhelming as I stand on a small hillside and peer at the distant horizon – perhaps 75 miles away. The empty space makes me feel tiny – like a dot in the middle of a huge plain.

This hill or more accurately mound sits on the eastern edge of Choibalsan – a medium-sized town a couple of dozen miles from the Chinese border in eastern Mongolia. From a distance, the town looks like any other Mongolian city.

A huge smokestack sits on the edge of town – belching white smoke into the atmosphere. This is the electric/heat plant. The plant burns tons of brown coal per day – generating electricity and supplying the town with hot water. Giant pipes snake from the plant and disappear underground. These pipes carry scalding water to businesses, restaurants, government buildings and residential apartments – where a gauge then regulates the temperature. The water circulates through radiators and the water pipes.

Central heating was a Soviet idea. Before the Russians came in the 1920's, most people lived in gers or small houses and each one had an individual heater that burned wood, dung and sometimes coal. The Soviets built multi-story apartment buildings and installed radiators, running water and electricity.

Since the fall of the Soviet Union and the arrival of the free-market, many of the first floor Soviet apartments have been converted into shops, office space, bars and restaurants. One eating establishment called Winners has added a patio for summer dining, a stone fireplace, a hand-carved wooden bar and modern track lighting. And the food isn't bad either. Oddly though – and I have found this to be the case only in

104

Choibalsan – almost every lunch place where I dine plays heavy metal music. Fortunately, each establishment has a place to "escape to" – individual private dining rooms or VIP rooms.

Restaurants are the only shops that are plentiful; I'm always amazed at how many supermarkets are in these towns. There are often five or six within less than a block – and it is like stepping back into time. All the food is behind the counter – stacked on floor to ceiling shelves. Huge wooden boxes contain delicious individually-wrapped candies from Russia. Bottles of Coke, Sprite and mineral water share space with two dozen brands of vodka and beer. One brand of Russian beer comes in a liter bottle – and is known among the expats as honey beer. Surprisingly, the hint of honey gives this beer a nice flavor.

Sitting off to one side of the room is a freezer or two – one is usually stuffed with cuts of meats while the other is filled with Popsicle's and ice cream cones. No, it's not Baskin Robbins, but Russian ice cream is quite delicious. And so are the Russian-made fruit juices. Personally, I find the "J-7" brand to be my favorite.

There is a mix of Russian, Chinese, Italian, Korean, German and Swiss products in stores across Mongolia – although the vast majority of products do come from Russia – including some familiar American-brand names: Colgate, Comet, Downy, Tide, Snickers and Mars -- all made in plants in Russia.

Just above the store may be a hotel. The rooms often range in quality, but for me, it's the bed that is most important and it's often in pretty bad shape. This is one reason I bring along a sleeping bag.

In Choibalsan, the hotel is new – with a pool table on the second floor – about three doors down from my room. Fortunately, the rooms are almost soundproof – and most importantly – the bed is comfortable and there is heat and hot water. As a bonus – there's cable TV – including one in English – The Disney Channel.

It's definitely luxurious compared to some of the other places I've stayed in Mongolia – where the water faucets hissed, the toilets gurgled all night and the mattress springs left indentations in my back.

Recently in Sukhbaatar City – north near the Russian border – the hotel room was clean and warm – and there was plenty of hot water. The problem was – there usually wasn't any cold water – which made it impossible to shower. The one shower I did manage to take when the cold water was turned on required getting on my knees in the prayer position in the tub because the shower nozzle was welded to a two-foot high water pipe.

And then there was the shower in Darkhan that had plastered tiles of naked women in various poses randomly etched into the wall. But the real shocker was the metal shower nozzle. When I touched it – I got an electrical shock.

That was the half-luxury room.

Unfortunately, the luxury room in Khenti Province had no hot water, but I had to pay extra for the shower and tub anyway. The receptionist informed me that they might have hot water in a few days and therefore she couldn't adjust the rate. Admittedly, it was a nice shower to look at; it had marble floors and brass-looking faucets.

I thought I had checked into the Hotel California in the town of Erdenet. I attempted to leave my room to go down to breakfast and the doorknob fell off in my hand. Some twenty minutes later, my driver rescued me.

My least expensive hotel room was four bucks – the most expensive was 25 dollars.

In UB, you obviously pay much more – and these hotels offer a wider variety of services to their clientele. My friend, Tracey, once stayed in one of the nicer UB hotels and she noticed that one of the services included massage. She called reception and was asked whether she wanted a health or medical massage. "I have a shoulder injury. What do you recommend," she asked. The receptionist informed her that she probably wanted a medical massage. She then asked Tracey "When and where would you like it?"

Tracey said "how about now in my room."

Fifteen minutes later there was a knock on her door and when Tracey opened it – two men step into the room and immediately dropped their pants and underwear. Tracey described them this way: "one was long and skinny and the other was short and fat."

After the initial shock – Tracey informed them there must be some mistake – that she needed a shoulder massage. "Oh," replied long and skinny, "you should have asked for the health massage!"

A few days later, Tracey and her boyfriend, Chris, walked into the hotel after returning from a trip to the countryside. As they placed their bags down at the reception desk – the bellhop came over to help them to their room. As they rode the elevator to the seventh floor – Tracey happened to notice the bellhop. "It was short and fat," she said. Tracey said she broke out in a huge grin – while short and fat began to giggle.

And then there was the young woman who walked into my ger in the middle of the night one night – flipped on the light and began speaking Mongolian. She didn't drop her pants, but she sat on the edge of my bed for 15 to 20 minutes – while I remained trapped in my birthday suit under the covers. She eventually gave up and left. She did know one English word. She mouthed "sorry" as she shut off the light and closed the door.

These kinds of hotel experiences are uniquely Mongolian and it's one of the reasons I enjoy traveling around this country. One never knows what to expect – each stop is an adventure.

Back on that small hillside just outside Choibalsan – I am surveying the vast landscape: the sun has just dropped over the horizon – turning the eastern sky reddish orange and a purplish pink. The outline of the city has changed dramatically in these few minutes – the buildings have become blackened rectangles and squares and that giant smokestack now resembles a sentinel – keeping watch over the city on the steppe.

January 17, 2004

The Blizzard Hike

The snow is stinging the area around my eyes so intensely I use my right hand as a shield as I hike my way across a vast plain east of Ulaanbaatar. Near white out conditions, heavy snowfall and wind gusts of nearly 60 miles an hour make the going slow.

Yet, the hike is exhilarating and there's no question – it's going to be memorable.

My four hiking mates and I had taken two taxis more than a dozen kilometers outside Ulaanbaatar and gotten dropped off on the flat plain that eventually became a tree covered hillside divided by a narrow river valley.

Now, as we hike south into the valley, I notice the clouds are getting darker by the minute. We keep moving further into the hills – crossing the frozen river. The light snow has covered the ice just enough to give our boots something to grasp, but in places the ice is treacherous and a couple of us slip and then crawl our way across the slippery surface.

As we hike along the river bank – the snow begins to get heavier, but the peacefulness seems to draw us deeper and deeper into the hills. The ice-covered river is surrealistic in that small cascades of water have seemingly frozen instantly. The thick ice forms a near solid ring around 70 and 80-year old trees – leaving huge cracks in the bark. It is almost like the ice and the trees are at war – and the ice is winning.

We find a giant log across the river and after dusting off the three inches or so of snow – we use it as our lunch table and chairs. As we eat fresh bread, cheese, apples and other fruits – we watch as the snow keeps getting heavier and the flakes bigger. We also have to keep turning our bodies away from the ever-increasing razor sharp winds.

It's a good place to turn back.

Making our way back down the trail, it continues to snow – harder and harder. The going is much slower on the way back because the snow is much deeper – perhaps seven inches.

It isn't until we step out of the narrow river valley back into the open plain that we really notice the force of the winds. It's unlike anything any of us have experienced – the blowing snow and high winds nearly knock us off our feet. The snow is blowing sideways into the right side of our faces. So, we line up side by side to try to shield each other as best we can. We can see perhaps ten feet in front of us – but fortunately we have a general idea of the direction we need to go to reach the main highway again.

The blowing snow begins to freeze on our clothing – and small chunks of ice begin to form on my eyelashes – affecting my vision. Removing my glove for less than ten seconds to wipe away the ice – my hand begins to turn red and the cold stings my fingers. It is difficult getting the glove back on – as it has frozen stiff – along with my scarf, face-mask and knit cap.

Surprisingly, I am not cold.

Hiking mate, Jim, however, is struggling – mainly because he isn't prepared. He tells us his head is freezing – and it's because, for fun, he had decided to wear a court jester's hat with tiny bells on the pointed ends. We will definitely be able to find him if he wonders off just by following the sound of the bells on the hat!

Jim's face is red from the icy winds – and his neck is exposed to cold because he doesn't have a scarf. In fact, he jokes that he didn't even bring one to Mongolia when he moved here seven months ago. But he sure needs one on this particular day -- and Gary, who had organized the hike, comes up with a practical solution. He pulls out an extra pair of long johns from his backpack and wraps them around Jim's neck and face to keep the wind out.

We keep moving – listening to the winds whistling across the power lines directly over our heads. Further along, we hear a train whistle and know we are getting closer to the highway. We can hear the train, but we can't see it through the thick blanket of fast-falling snow.

Still further, Jim, who is now a much happier camper with those long johns around his neck and face, reaches down into the snow and pulls out a cow's skull. He holds it in his left arm like a football – striking a pose in the blizzard as I snap a photograph.

Suddenly, we see movement – shadows in the distance cars and trucks. The highway is just ahead and we make our way up the embankment and onto the roadway – where we flag down a taxi and all five of us cram into the tiny Korean made car and slowly make our way back into the city.

In one sense, I am disappointed the adventure is over. I love the feeling of not knowing exactly where I am – the sense of not being in control – wondering how long it might take to find the highway. I guess one reason I enjoyed the blizzard experience so much is the fact that I was cozy in my warm clothing. I always bring along extra layers and a face-mask when I go into the woods on a winter day. You just never know what might happen.

February 15, 2004

Homeward Bound

I was thinking I might get lucky and the seat next to me will remain empty and as the last of the air travelers file onto the plane in Tokyo – things are looking pretty good. I just might just get a big break as I continue my 20 hour flight from Ulaanbaatar to Washington, DC with this stopover in Japan.

As I begin to get comfortable -- stretching out my long legs and raising the seats' arm rest – a young man with close-cropped blonde hair suddenly appears – looking as if he's in a daze. He hovers over me without saying a word – until finally, he points at the empty window seat and says "I sit there."

Once he squeezes his six-foot frame past me and into 38-A he turns to me and asks, "So how long were you in Japan?"

"Two hours," I reply.

"And you?" I ask – not really caring, but trying to be friendly.

"About 24 hours," he replies with pain in his face and voice.

The 20-something begins describing how he'd flown in from Fort Lauderdale, Florida this time yesterday. He'd filled out the Japanese immigration form and had written down the names of ten people he planned to visit – including his girlfriend – who he'd met while stationed in the US Navy in Japan three years ago.

As it turns out, almost everyone on his list, including his Filipino girlfriend was an illegal alien living in Japan. And to make matters even worse – he had told the immigration officer that he wanted to find work and settle down in Japan.

So, in a matter of minutes – this young man sitting next to me had managed to get himself kicked out of Japan and had unknowingly ratted out his friends living illegally in the country and had even provided addresses for each one. Now, on the plane, he tells me he feels guilty about what he'd done – and describes himself as "incredibly stupid."

I just nod.

After our plane reaches cruising altitude, Brian, who never told me his name, but showed me his passport and documents stamped by the Japanese immigration officer, calls a flight attendant – and orders the first of what must have been 20 rum and cokes. He is careful to ask a different flight attendant each time – so as not to get cut off. Eventually, they catch on – and offer him Baileys instead.

He's holding his liquor pretty well – slumping in his seat for the last two hours of the nearly 12 hour flight to Chicago. But during the journey he made nearly a dozen trips to the restroom.

After his first trip to the toilet, I stand up to stretch my legs and wander to the back – where a drama is playing out between two or three passengers and a flight attendant.

The smell of cigarette smoke is pouring from the toilet and everyone is trying to remember who has just used the facilities. One of the male flight attendants searches the trash can for the evidence, but a passenger comments "no one would be that stupid – it got flushed, no doubt." The attendant patiently replies "you'd be surprised." But there is no butt – and no one seems to recall who had just used the toilet, but I have my suspicions – having smelled cigarette smoke on my seat mate.

Returning to my seat – and without accusing him, I tell Brian that someone narrowly missed getting caught smoking in the restroom – and that the flight attendants will call federal authorities if it happens again. Of course, he denies it.

Not an hour later, he gets busted – and then, amazingly, two hours later – Brian gets caught again.

He's incredibly lucky.

Two flight attendants come to our seats and very sternly warn him that if he gets caught one more time – federal marshals will meet the plane in Chicago and that he'll be arrested and face charges. Luckily, the alcohol eventually put him to sleep – and he wakes up just as the plane touches down at O'Hare.

March 27, 2004

Return to Mongolia

It is twilight when my plane touches down at the airport outside UB. It is 10 p.m. and still daylight. I'm experiencing white nights – when the sun never really sets in the northern climes. It just sits on the horizon.

Newly fallen rain makes the wheels of the jeep hiss as the driver slowly makes his way past the power and heat plants – with their tall smokestacks -- out on the western side of town. We turn right onto the main drag – Peace Avenue – and now it begins to get a bit darker. Pedestrians inch their way across the busy streets – my driver weaves past them – at times narrowly missing the dark figures standing on the yellow line in the middle of the street as gas fumes float in the air just above the asphalt.

Familiar smells fill my nostrils – smoke from the grills of vendors – who are selling (shorlog) shish-ka-bobs on the sidewalks. A groaning bus slides past us – belching blue smoke. The rain gives the night air an earthy smell.

I had left Mongolia nearly three months earlier, in the middle of a frigid winter. Tonight, the air feels warm. I'm wearing a short-sleeve shirt and the breeze feels refreshing on my face.

As a result of the seemingly endless winter, I have forgotten how much I had enjoyed the previous Mongolian summer.

Next morning, I awake at 6 am and head for the gym. It is a perfect morning for a walk. The air feels fresh – and I can see forever. The distant green hills overlooking the city are shining in the morning sun. I meet only a handful of people and each greet me warmly – it's as if we are sharing something special this morning. I've never felt more alive and in the moment. For me, this morning in late June makes up for all those icy streets and sidewalks and long nights of below zero cold.

My return to Mongolia coincides with Parliamentary elections – just seven days away. As we cruise toward my apartment that first night, almost every billboard is a political poster – many with candidates posing with popular Mongolian musicians – some of whom are paid to play music at political concerts. Some singers and entertainers might earn as much as $1000 per concert. Mongolian entertainers always look forward to elections because it means extra money for them.

By far, most of the posters feature members of the ruling communist party or Mongolian People's Revolutionary Party – others are members of smaller parties – including the Democratic opposition. The MPRP is considered the heavy favorite since it controls the national television and radio networks. It is difficult for other party candidates to get even a couple of minutes of airtime on state run media.

At the gym a few days after my arrival, but before the election, I meet the Russian Ambassador. He asks me how many seats I think the opposition candidates will win. I respond: "ten." He looks at me a moment and says, "You're very pessimistic."

He's right. The democratic opposition captured nearly half the 76 parliament seats.

Voting is done manually with voters circling the name of the candidate on a paper ballot. Once the selections are made, the voter drops the ballot in a box. After voting, the voter presents his left index finger to an election official who puts a small dot of ink on the cuticle. This is to keep someone from voting twice.

At the polling place I visited in Ulaanbaatar, observers from each of the parties were on hand to watch for irregularities. Two monitors from different parties told me they had observed nothing out of the ordinary.

Separately, they told me that by mid-afternoon more than 1,000 voters had filed through this particular polling place. I observed a small, but steady stream of voters during the 20 minutes I spent there.

Ganhuyag, who came to pick me up at the airport that first night, tells me a lot of things get repaired just before an election. I notice that a giant pothole that had been in the alley near my apartment had been paved over. Newly installed water sprinkler systems have turned the weeds around the Prime Minister's residence a dark green, trucks with huge blaring loudspeakers cruise the alleyways and a young boy knocks on my door and hands me a political flyer. When I accept it, he grins and excitedly says in perfect English "thanks."

The next morning, on my way to work, I notice that all the usual traffic cops have disappeared. Usually, they are out in force each morning, busily writing tickets. This morning, not a one is in sight.

Later that afternoon at my office, one of my Mongolian coworkers tells me that it is unfortunate that elections aren't held once a month or so – he says if that were the case "more things might get done around this country."

June 28, 2004

A Sheep Led to Slaughter

He has the skill of a surgeon as he placed the four-inch knife blade against the abdomen of the sheep and makes a four-inch incision. There is no blood. The sheep instantly raises its head – a wide-eyed look on its face. I want to turn my face away, but I can't.

I watch as the herder sticks his hand and part of his forearm into the incision, locates a main artery and severs it. The sheep struggles – crying for its life and desperately fighting a losing battle. I watch as life slowly drains from the animal.

I have never seen this type of slaughter before. I've been told it was instantaneous and that the animal doesn't suffer. In this case, this sheep struggled for a good 60 seconds. Later, I was told this particular slaughter didn't go as smoothly as most.

Mongolians have slaughtered their sheep this way for centuries.

Moments after this animal is slaughtered, the butcher and another guy dressed the sheep under a shade tree by the Tuul River – about 60 kilometers southeast of Ulaanbaatar, the capital. The butcher performs his job efficiently – first removing the hide which slips off like the peel from an orange. Next he makes another incision, carefully removing the intestines and the stomach – which are a bit bigger than a basketball. Next the organs are removed – all the while there's very little blood. By the time he reaches the rib cage – a small pool of blood has gathered, but he uses a plastic cup to dip it out and pour it into a plastic bag.

As the butcher cuts up the meat, nearby, two guys have built a small wood fire – with round river pebbles as the base. A three-foot high metal jug with a sealed lid that resembles an old-fashioned milk container is placed over the fire. About one gallon of water is poured in – along with salt and herbs. Next, those now-sizzling hot river pebbles are added to the jug – followed by small whole potatoes, onions and carrots. Finally small chunks of meat are placed inside the container – and still more hot rocks. The jug is then sealed up for about half an hour – the fire is stoked and steam escapes through the not-so-airtight lid.

The dish is called horhog – and it's delicious. It's the second time I have helped prepare this particular dish. The first time had been two months earlier in a beautiful ice-filled valley in the South Gobi. Ice can be seen there almost year round. On that particular day in June – it was cold after the sun disappeared behind the mountain – and we used those hot rocks from the pot to keep warm – tossing the stones from one hand to the other.

Horhog is definitely my favorite Mongolian dish. The meat and vegetables have incredible flavors – and the meat is extremely tender.

Horhog is often eaten as a picnic dish – and on both occasions the surroundings have been spectacular. On this day, I'm joined by about 30 or so colleagues from work. We swim in the nearby cold, but exhilarating waters of the Tuul, play tug of war, (my team won both matches) rest in the grass on the sloping banks of the river and watch the puffy white clouds create intense shadows on the nearby mountains.

We work off lunch by playing volleyball, jumping rope and enjoying a friendly hand or two of hearts.

No one wants to leave this peaceful place, but we eventually have to climb aboard our contrary and rickety old city bus – and make our way back into town. Along the way, my western colleague and I are entertained by our Mongolian work mates – who sing drinking songs and young pioneer songs – songs from the old communist days – when young people boarded buses and headed to the countryside for two weeks of vacation.

August 7, 2004

Voting Absentee from Mongolia

My election ballot had arrived 24 hours ago. The FEDEX package looked a bit frayed around the edges, but that was probably because it took a wrong turn in Beijing.

I had been tracking the package via the Internet since it had left the East Coast of the U.S. some ten days ago. The first stop was FEDEX headquarters in Memphis, then to Anchorage, Tokyo and on to Beijing. It sat in Beijing for three days and was supposed to be placed on the two-hour flight up to Ulaanbaatar. Instead, my ballot wound up in Subic Bay, The Philippines for 24 hours – before being sent to Seoul for another 24 hours.

I joked to a colleague that my ballot was on an East Asian tour – and that just about the only place it hadn't visited yet was North Korea.

The morning of October 14, I decided to check the FEDEX website again just to be amused. Where would my ballot be this day? As I peered into my laptop screen, I noticed the package was still at the airport in Seoul. But it turns out, the ballot had even given the FEDEX tracker the slip.

It wasn't in Seoul anymore – it was directly in front of me. My colleague, Onchik, was holding it – and as I turned away from my laptop screen – I recognized the familiar lettering on the package.

I was overjoyed.

I lifted Onchik completely off the floor and twirled her about the room as I clung to my ballot. She stands less than five feet tall – and we have worked together for almost a year – but as I twirled her she seemed to notice for the first time – my six foot, two inch frame. She smiled and giggled and said "you're so tall."

It had cost 80 bucks to get my ballot to Mongolia, but in the end FEDEX agreed to refund the money. My ballot is due back in Maryland on Monday, October 18 – unless it takes another detour – maybe to Taiwan this time.

October 15, 2004

Losing Everything and Finding Most of It Again

It's your worst nightmare: losing your passport, credit cards, your wallet and your apartment keys. It happened to an Australian colleague of mine a few days ago after a night of partaking in the local culture: lots of shots of vodka.

It was around 2 a.m. when she noticed her bag was missing. After retracing her steps as best she could remember, she headed back to her apartment, and it was then she realized her keys were in the missing bag, too.

Her landlord was none too pleased to receive a call in the middle of the night – particularly from someone who had been drinking heavily, but he promptly showed up. Unfortunately, he didn't have an extra key to her apartment, so she lay on a blanket on his floor the rest of the night.

It was the following morning that I learned of her misfortune. Somehow, she hadn't lost her mobile phone. My colleague sent me a text message – asking for advice.

We agreed to meet in an hour and retrace her steps once again.

She had warned me that she was in a bad way in more ways than one. She had a pounding headache, severely bloodshot eyes and her hair was in knots. She declined the offer of a shower – wanting to get back to the last place she'd remembered being the night before: The Chinggis Pub and Restaurant. (Mongolians spell "Genghis," as in Khan, as "Chinggis.")

After a search of the trash cans, cloakroom and booths – it's clear the bag isn't in the pub.

Next: cancel the credit cards. (She had forgotten to mention them until this point.)

I have to say that if a person is going to lose all their documents and credit cards – Mongolia is probably one of the best places to do it.

Identity theft is almost unheard of in this country. And most people don't use credit cards anyway. In fact, several colleagues and friends have lost their documents here and nine out of ten times they've gotten them back. It's not always easy, though.

Sometimes, you have to pay a reward – maybe $15 sometimes more, but chances are you'll get your stuff back – most of it anyway.

My colleague is somewhat comforted by my statistics, but still skeptical as I would probably be, too. We begin by going to a place in the city center where you can make a report about your missing items – and the announcement is then broadcast on all the local radio and television stations. It costs about 20 cents a word.

Thirty-six hours later, the phone call comes in.

The voice on the other end of the line says: I have your bag and all the stuff inside. I'll call tomorrow at 9 a.m. The next morning, my colleague is a relieved wreck -- pacing around the office – clock watching. 9:10 – no call. 9:30 no call, 10:00 still no call. Finally, at ten-thirty, the guy calls back and says he will need a reward of $100.

The receptionist who took the call tells him that's an outrageous amount, but he says it's either the money or no bag. He then gives instructions to meet in front of the circus in 15 minutes.

The whole thing reminds me of a prisoner exchange.

The guy shows up 30 minutes late with the bag – and he has brought along a little insurance – a buddy who looks like a sumo wrestler.

After a few minutes of negotiations, the exchange is made. My colleague pays the guy a total of $80.

Mr. Sumo stands a few feet away making sure everyone understands there is to be no funny stuff.

October 19, 2004

First Day of Cold

November 9 is the beginning of the slip and slide period – the time Mongolians begin to shuffle their feet to keep from falling on the ice and snow. An inch or two of snow the previous evening has shrouded the city of Ulaanbaatar in a beautiful mask of white – covering years of neglect.

However, with the temperature several degrees below freezing, the snow becomes the foundation of what will eventually be several inches of ice on sidewalks and streets -- ice that won't melt until spring.

I have been anxious about this day for more than a month. Last year – that first layer of ice came in early October – and I remember the dread as I stepped onto it for the first time. It was a fear of falling – and a deeper fear of crossing the street. The ice made the game of chicken between pedestrians and motorists much more dangerous.

Cars and buses almost never stop for pedestrians – even in cross walks. Now, it was impossible to run across the street – and it was equally impossible for cars and buses to even consider slowing down – with the ice and their bald tires.

As I step outside this November morning, my feet crunch the new fallen snow. I try to walk in places that had not been trampled down so as not to fall. Shopkeepers are out with their brooms – removing the snow from their entrances. But that creates its own hazard. The sidewalk tiles are extremely slippery when wet or when a little snow remains on them. One must walk with extreme caution on these polished tiles.

As I make my way to the busy intersection, I notice the red light is working today. But the street is packed with snow and looks hazardous. As the "walk" sign starts blinking, I step slowly from the curb into the street. A yellow cab comes driving up and scoots to a stop just two feet from me. I quickly glance at the driver and then resume my careful trek across the icy street.

One of the good things about the ice and snow is that it's easier to spot open manholes. I have heard all sorts of stories about people falling into them – particularly at night.

A Mongolian friend described how her brother narrowly missed falling into one -- saved by a homeless guy who was popping his head out of the manhole just as her brother was stepping on it. Instead of falling in, her brother literally stepped on the guy's head.

Above the streets as ice forms on the trolley car wires, blue arcs of electricity shoot from the wires as the trolley burps along its route. At times, the cable connecting the trolley to the power line comes loose – forcing the driver's assistant to climb on top of the bus to reconnect the wires. I always cringe when I see this – fearing I will witness an electrocution.

November 9, 2004

Homeless in Ulaanbaatar

He's pounding on the metal door of my apartment with both fists calling my name. His voice echoes through the stairwell.

Sometimes, I open the door, most times, I don't.

It's a difficult situation.

Bataa lives in the stairwell, near the radiator – sleeping on a piece of cardboard. He hangs his sweatshirts on the hot radiator pipes. His shoes and felt blanket are stacked in the corner.

I have tried to find him a place to live, but he always winds up back in the stairwell. He looks to be anywhere in age from ten to 14, but a lack of good nutrition has affected his growth. Bataa tells me he is 20 – and that no one will take him in.

He's just one of dozens of people – mostly boys and young men – living on the streets of UB. In the winter time, most go underground – into the manholes – where the heating pipes that snake through the city keep them warm.

I never give Bataa money, but often provide him with food – usually fruit. He is very appreciative. He has a broad smile and surprisingly has a bit of a gleam in his eyes. That's very surprising given his situation.

He speaks a few words of English. He rubs his stomach and says "hungry." Other times, he rubs his throat. I take that to mean he would like something to drink. Still other times, he rubs his head and frowns – and mouths the words: "head hurts." I give him aspirin. He has told me on several occasions that he doesn't have anyone – no siblings, no parents, no one.

One never knows the real situation.

A German family with three young children lives in the only other occupied apartment in the building. They live on the third floor – just above me. They had adopted Bataa when he first moved in last August. They fed him regularly, but he got very demanding. He started pounding on their door at all hours of the night screaming for food. The family eventually put up a metal gate just outside my stairwell to keep him from climbing up to their front door.

It's a dilemma.

I don't want Bataa to starve, but I also don't want him to come to depend on me either. It's a situation we all face each time we encounter a homeless person.

For Mongolia, it's a relatively new problem – homelessness wasn't really an issue during the Soviet years.

December 8, 2004

The Deer Stones

The beige Russian jeep bounces along the snowy steppe in north central Mongolia as the driver keeps the front wheels in the two snow-packed tracks. The jeep seems to be keeping rhythm to the Mongolian music playing on a cassette deck welded beneath the steel dashboard.

The music is playing in the background as my five companions and I chat. Suddenly, Baagi points to a long rounded mountain range ahead of us and says there is a legend that the range was once a large serpent that was drinking all the water in the nearby river. Something had to be done or the province would turn into a vast desert. So, a local man sliced off the serpent's head and became an instant hero.

As we drive closer to the edge of the mountain range – a large chunk of the mountain is clearly separated from the long range – as if someone had, indeed, sliced right through the mountain.

We drive halfway through the gap in the mountain and stop.

We climb out of the jeep and up the side of the serpent's head – as Baagi points to our destination: a small cave in the side of the rock. That, he says, is where the spine of the snake had been.

As we stand in the cave, our driver pulls out a bottle of vodka and uses an orange tail light from the jeep as a cup. We pass the tail light full of vodka around at least twice before the driver empties the last few drops onto the rocks as an offering.

The temperature is hovering around minus 15, so the vodka definitely warms us up as we climb back down toward the jeep.

Our ultimate destination is another 10 kilometers across the steppe – a large field of "deer stones." They're rocks planted in the ground like tombstones – standing anywhere from five to eight feet high. They were erected sometime around 3500 BC and are believed to mark burial sites.

There are more than a dozen of these stone sentinels standing among us – and around them are a similar number of huge mounds of earth – also believed to be burial sites. A local historian, Nyamaa, however, tells me that the deer stones and the mounds are not believed to be from the same period. It's unclear which is the oldest.

The stones are a work of art. On the surfaces are hand-carved figures of deer, the sun, the moon, knives, bows and arrows and one even has a human face. These stones are believed to be dedicated to tribal chiefs and warriors – the more symbols on a stone – the more important the person was.

In recent years, at least one of the stones has been sliced in three chunks – and several others have been sprayed with a chemical to highlight the symbols. But the chemical has caused the stone's face to disintegrate – and the symbols are literally crumbling away.

We have the site to ourselves on this particular day – as the sentinels cast long shadows on the virgin snow while the sun attempts in vain to warm the subzero plain.

On the way back into town, two of my companions serenade us with beautiful local songs – handed down over the ages by one of the six ethic groups living in the Khovsgul area.

It was Christmas caroling – Mongolian-style on this day before Christmas.

December 24, 2004

Landing in a Snow Storm

The 20-something year old Russian-AN-24 plane bumps along as it descends toward Moron in Khovsgul province in a driving snowstorm. The sun had set hours ago and all we can see is blackness through the windows as we descend. Then, 20 seconds before we actually touch down, we see a few lights and the virgin snow on the concrete runway. It covers the strip and everything else – and it was still snowing.

I knew what I was getting into before I boarded the MIAT flight in Ulaanbaatar. The community radio station director in Moron had called and told us that a snow storm was blowing through, but he added it should be gone by the time we arrive.

I had called him to check the weather after Aero Mongolia, a privately run commercial airliner, had canceled its flight to Khovsgul, but good old state-run MIAT wasn't about to let a snow storm stop it from making its regularly scheduled flight.

I have flown MIAT dozens of time during my two Knight fellowships in Mongolia. It's the fastest way to get to my workshops at the half dozen or so community radio stations broadcasting from remote corners of this vast country. Driving is not an option unless you have three or four days just to get there. The roads are mostly dirt trails across the steppe.

I was in Moron on this snowy night to conduct a workshop on how to develop interviewing skills. I also planned to show my journalism colleagues how to extract short, but descriptive sound bites from interviews for use in radio news stories. I also wanted to show them how to use natural sound in storytelling and how to put it all together using digital editing software.

The next morning, I give my student, Tsend-Ochir, a 35-year-old editor, an assignment: find an interesting candidate and interview the person for an audio diary. The story must be told by the individual and the reporter must make use of lots of natural sound.

Tsend-Ochir has a candidate in mind.

He, my translator Ganaa, and I walk about one kilometer to the edge of town to the ger district – and after a few wrong turns we find the right alleyway and knock on a green door built into a quarter acre fenced compound. Eventually, an elderly man steps from his ger – which sits in the middle of the fenced area – and he motions for us to come inside.

Sandajgav, who tells us he's 82, has a long gray beard and a friendly face. After he sits down, he pours each of us a purplish homemade concoction that has a bitter smell and earthy taste. Among the ingredients: turnips and raisins.

Tsend-Ochir is a little nervous about how to start the interview, so I suggest he ask Sandajgav to talk about the first thing he does after waking up. "I like to step outside my ger and watch the sun come up," he says. Tsend-Ochir picks up on his answer and asks about the garden space just outside the ger. Sandajgav tells him it was a summer hobby and adds that staying active and drinking that purplish liquid are two secrets to his long life.

As Tsend-Ochir's minidisk recorder continues to roll – Sandajgav pulls out a home-made chess set and dominoes. He likes to play these games with friends during the long, cold winters. He tells us his favorite board game is "Dame" – a game that's played like checkers. Sandajgav uses plastic bottle caps as the game pieces and a hand-painted piece of cardboard for the checker board.

In my workshops across Mongolia, I have found this audio diary exercise to be very helpful in teaching beginner journalists how to ask follow up questions because the atmosphere is usually relaxed and the conversation is usually more natural. Since the reporter is asked to find his or her own subject, there is often a genuine curiosity – and that usually leads to good questions.

Audio diaries also get the reporter to think in terms of how to humanize their stories through the use of first person narrative and natural sound. These elements were something that I noticed was often lacking in stories when I first arrived in Mongolia as a Knight Fellow in June 2003.

As a reward to the stations for their work on the audio diaries, I'm able to get small grants from the US Embassy in Ulaanbaatar. The grants are in the form of equipment – everything from headphones and microphones to minidisk recorders and flash discs.

The flash discs allow the reporter to copy the program from the station computer and take it to the local Internet café so it can be uploaded to a website that I had set up so that the stories can be shared with other stations.

In the months since the start of my fellowship, I have witnessed a huge change in the way stories are covered. For instance, reporters at the community station in Darkhan, Mongolia's second largest city, have produced a 10-part series on how to start and maintain a small business. Each episode uses anecdotes, natural sound and examples from individuals who are attempting to launch or who have already started a business.

I was able to secure a grant of $2000 from two organizations to help fund this project. Most of the grant money was used to buy much-needed broadcast equipment: microphones, a minidisk recorder, headphones and cables.

In the South Gobi, a small team of reporters at a station called Gobi Wave Radio produced a five-part series that targeted the herder population. Using sound bites from herders, the reporters wanted to educate livestock owners about the advantages of diversification.

More than a dozen herders were interviewed for the project. Some described how they had lost all their livestock in a severe drought and were forced to give up herding and move to urban areas to become cab drivers or trash collectors. Others described how they diversified by making furniture, growing vegetables or making felt, allowing them to generate enough extra income to survive the tough times. Still others told of how they formed cooperatives to ease their financial losses during severe weather.

Gobi Wave received two $500 grants to produce the program as well as a $75 travel allowance in order to visit herder families in the vast Gobi region.

In the days before the end of the year, three community stations, in Selenge, Darkhan and Dornod, produced a multi-part series on HIV/AIDS. The stories were aimed at clearing up misconceptions about the disease – misconceptions that the reporters discovered are sometimes held even by health care professionals in the countryside of Mongolia.

Each of the programs is being aired locally by the community radio stations – as well as nationally on Mongol Radio. So, the impact is substantial.

Back in the studio in Khovsgul, Tsend-Ochir has finished editing his audio diary on the elderly writer. It opens with natural sound of the writer striking the keys of his old manual typewriter as he describes how he enjoys writing in the morning – after walking outside to watch the sun come up and tending his vegetable garden. As he describes his routine, the typewriter sound fades away and the listener hears the crunching sound of footsteps in the icy snow. Later, he talks about his hobby of making knives. As he speaks the sound of hammering and grinding slowly fades in under his voice.

Tsend-Ochir has created a five minute movie that put his listener right there in the ger with the 82-year-old Sandajgav.

He was painting images with sound.

Author's Note: *The Soviet-built Antonov AN-24 44-seat twin turboprop used by MIAT have been retired and now reside in a museum in Ulanbaatar.*

January 5, 2005

Epilogue

It has been nearly seven years since I left Mongolia in the late spring of 2005. Yet, more than half a dozen years later, my memories of life there are still vivid – the visits to the communal saunas in remote villages to warm up from the sub-zero weather, walking on the steppe as grasshoppers dance and crackle in the tall grass around me, the horseback rides through cold rivers and seemingly endless countryside and, of course, the warm hospitality of the Mongolian people.

My work, in the area of media development, has taken me to more than half a dozen different countries since my time in Mongolia. Each has had its own special qualities, but Mongolia has always been the standard by which I have measured the other places. This may sound unfair in one sense, but it's probably because Mongolia was the first place outside the United States that I lived for any significant amount of time.

Mongolia was the beginning of my journey beyond my homeland. It was the place where I discovered that I enjoyed the nomadic life – moving from place to place – experiencing the local culture, sharing a bit of my own and making new friends along the way.

I write this epilogue from my home in the mountains of western North Carolina where I have spent the last 14 months hiking and relaxing – preparing for my next nomadic journey – wherever it may be.

June 2012

Made in the USA
San Bernardino, CA
29 November 2018